TO OUR CHILDREN SAM, LOLA AND TESSA.

SECRETS TO PROGRESSIVE
SURFING

BY **DIDIER PITER** | PHOTOGRAPHY **BERNARD TESTEMALE**

F O R E W O R D

To be a complete surfer, I think it's important to be good in all conditions and be ready for anything that is thrown your way. I grew up in Florida surfing small, choppy waves. Some people are lucky to grow up where the surf is consistent and there are perfectly groomed point breaks. I always wished that was me but I had to make do with what was thrown at us back home. In Florida, basically we learned to surf in a quick way. The waves are short and messy generally so your style has to suit that approach.

But how does that translate to bigger and cleaner waves and what are the benefits and difficulties in doing that? How can you take that approach to other places and what can you learn from others that can help you? I always felt it was a benefit to learn quickly on small waves rather than in big scary surf where it's hard to have control. From there you can build up to larger waves and take a more radical approach to maneuvers. If you were to teach a child to play golf, I'm sure it's easier for them to make a short putt than to drive the ball 300 meters down the fairway so you have to start slowly, and I had no choice because even the biggest waves in Florida are still small by most standards. Start slowly, build confidence by using the right equipment and take note of people around you and what they are doing that can help you. Learn by watching, but also lead by your own approach and example once you have something really figured out. Usually once you feel that way, you have something to learn again so you start from the beginning and the cycle repeats, but more quickly this time.

Each person has a different path they wish to follow. I have always loved the challenge of competition, but in surfing nowadays there are so many directions you can go. You can just freesurf or you can follow big waves and either paddle or tow. You can try and be a tour pro or get a job in the industry where you can go on surf trips for the rest of your life. Maybe you're a hippie and just want to travel and not have a job. I would recommend cooking and massage because wherever you go you can still find work.

Surfers, I find, are probably as true to themselves as any people and at the end of the day the whole idea is to try and catch the best waves you can for what you like to do. Don't stray from that objective... and give a wave to someone else sometimes even if you're the one in the perfect place for it. You'll appreciate the next one much more.

Just a small note on competition. For me, it's hard not to continue competing even when I just want to get away from the crowds and the constant battle of proving yourself. We get to make a living traveling the world doing what we love, and the more waves we catch and photos we get, the better off we generally are in our careers. Competition can bring out the best and worst of the human spirit. It can show you what you're made of, what you didn't know you had inside, and help you accomplish things you didn't even believe you could do. Or it can smash your confidence into millions of pieces. I've had some of my greatest memories from competing, but I hope to never think it's what makes me who I am as a person... it's just something I do and I happen to be pretty good at it.

Surfing is a never-ending challenge, requiring commitment to improving and learning, and is the most exciting thing I know of.
I hope all people get to feel that in life on some level. We have been blessed with a great experience here on this planet. I'm sure that Bernard's photos and Didier's texts will bring that to life for everyone reading this book.
Thanks for taking the time to read and I hope you get some good waves today.

KELLY SLATER

(INTRO)

The origins of surfing go back centuries, to the moment one Polynesian found pleasure riding waves and made the ocean a playground. Nowadays, surfing is a multi-billion dollar industry, counting millions of surfers across the globe.

Beyond a simple sporting act, surfing keeps fascinating more and more people and has become a true way of life, organised around the ocean. From the ancient Hawaiians to the third millennium surfer much has changed, but one sacred thing perpetuates through time, the pure pleasure of playing with a wave's energy.

The goal of this book is to share our experience and passion, and to give you, the reader as much information and as many tools as possible, to grasp the unique and timeless feeling of riding waves.

The book explains all fundamentals key to your progression, without forgetting the essential element - the wave.

Sport, passion, way of life... whatever your approach, we hope these pages will get you stoked to go surfing and enlighten your path in doing so.

Thank you for surfing with us on these pages.

CONTENTS

1.
UNDERSTANDING WAVES

Surfing starts with the wave, the essential element of your pleasure and progression.

The wave is a result of complex natural phenomena. Here you are, facing this moving liquid mass, ready to break after traveling for thousands of miles. It's time for you to adapt, to feel, to play. Without the wave, there can be no surfing. But with it, everything becomes possible. Whether a beginner at your local beach, or an expert out at the infamous Teahupoo, the principals are the same - the wave makes the surfer. Understanding it and adapting to it is your passport to progression and to maximum pleasure.

WAVE GENESIS

SWELL

Waves are born in atmospheric low-pressure systems, which blow storm winds over the ocean surface.

If the winds blow strong and long enough, they create waves that follow the wind's dominant direction.

Wave size depends on the wind speed, duration and distance over which it blows, known as 'fetch'. When strong and far enough from the coast, storm winds allow waves to organise and grow into swell. The longer the wave period (time interval between two waves) the further the swell will travel. When observing swell breaking at the shore, the period indicates how far the swell has traveled.

Short period swell (less than 7 second period): Generated close to the coast.
Medium period swell (7-11 second period): Generated hundreds of miles away.
Long period swell (above 11 second period): Generated from far out in the deep ocean.

BOTTOM EFFECTS

Swells move through deep water largely unhindered until a certain depth where they 'feel' the bottom, when friction between wave motion and the seabed starts slowing and bending the swell.

When the bottom sufficiently slows the wave base, it rises and steepens until a critical point when it breaks forward.

From this point, the breaking wave is born, and surfing is possible.

An infinity of underwater bottom shapes, affected by different swell sizes, periods and directions create an infinity of wave types.

Mushy waves: When the sea bottom is flat and gently shallows to the shore, waves break smoothly spilling over themselves, providing the ideal situation to learn surfing.

Hollow waves: When the swell goes from deep to rapidly shallowing waters, the wave face becomes concave and suddenly projects itself powerfully forward. These waves require both commitment and a high skill level to ride, and give the surfer the best sensations.

WIND

Not only does the wind generate waves far out in the ocean, it also affects breaking wave quality on shorelines.

Onshore wind: Creates a messy, choppy water surface hard to deal with whether paddling or surfing. Pushed from behind, the waves get flattened and scrambled. Blowing weak to moderate, the effects are slight. Once blowing stronger, it complicates the ride.
Offshore wind: Smoothes and organises the sea surface. Blowing into the wave and holding breaking up, the wave breaks in shallower water and becomes more hollow. Weak to moderate offshore winds create ideal surfing conditions.

Cross-shore wind: Often creates chops and complicates the ride.
Glassy: Without wind, waves get glassy and easier to ride.

TIDE

Tidal changes can create a wave or make it disappear, because each spot needs the right depth to break properly. A perfect beach break at mid-tide might not exist any more three hours later at high tide. The tide book is the surfer's best friend in regions with large tidal ranges, giving both tide times and heights.

+ TIP

Do not miss another session.
Study the coastline of your surfing region, and regularly analyse swell and wind forecasts on specialised websites.
Pay attention to size, direction and period of each swell, and check their influence on your favorite spots at different tides.
With this understanding you will prepare your sessions better, and choose the right spot for each swell and wind.

Useful websites:
www.windguru.cz   www.magicseaweed.com
www.surfline.com   www.buoyweather.com
etc.

At beach breaks, waves break over a sand bottom. The sandbanks are like bumps that make the waves break. Each beach counts many, with some visible at low tide. Some will last months, while others just hours.

A constantly shifting sandbank suggests unpredictable and random surf conditions. Banks appear and disappear according to storms, currents and swell directions.

Even if a sandbank is shaped to produce perfect waves, other elements come into play for the perfect beachbreak session:

- An offshore wind to smooth the wave face and make waves hollow.
- Swell size, period and direction suited to the sandbank shape.
- Tide, having the right water depth over the sandbank.

This ephemeral aspect and state of perpetual change is the magic of surfing beach breaks, requiring the surfer to be in tune with the elements and constantly in the quest for the right sandbank at that magic moment.

Generally, beach breaks offer ideal conditions for beginners. Paddling out and coming in are usually pretty easy, and wipeouts are generally less dangerous on sand than rocks or coral.

Longshore current: This is related to the swell direction, which gives rise to significant longshore movements of water (parallel to the shore). For example, northwest swells create southbound currents along a west-facing coast.

Rip current: After a set of waves, a large volume of water runs up the beach and accumulates close to shore. In order for it to escape, a rip current running out to sea establishes itself (perpendicular to the shore) using the deep water channels between

sandbanks. This current separates the different sandbanks that create waves.

A surfer can use rips to get to the peak or to position himself for catching waves.

DANGERS

The bottom: Be careful when falling.

Shorebreaks: A wave that breaks directly onto sand at the water's edge. It can be dangerously powerful, especially at high tide. Exit the wave before it reaches the shorebreak.

Currents: Especially strong on big swells, and at certain tides. Always be careful and pick a fixed point on the beach for position. Once in the surf zone, regularly check it to evaluate current strength and reposition yourself, if necessary. Never fight against a strong current; take a wave in to reposition yourself or walk up the beach. If there are no waves breaking, let the current take you out until its effect weakens, then paddle to the beach.

Famous beach breaks:

Puerto Escondido (Mexico), Black's (California) La Gravière (France), Supertubos (Portugal).

✚ TIP

With a tide book, plan a day at the beach. Observe the effects of tide on your spot and wave quality. Over the tide, you'll notice that waves change, peaks move, currents increase or lessen, and that each sandbank works at different moments.

Repeat this exercise at different beach breaks. These observations will help build the instincts and experience to be surfing the right place at the right time.

POINT BREAK

Point breaks are found at a bend or protrusion along the coastline that creates specific waves, where swells bend in concave refraction, wrapping around the point and in to shore. The point break's relatively even or uniform configuration makes the waves break in the same spot and in one direction. This simplifies paddling around the waves and positioning on the peak. The more the swell refracts from its original direction, the smaller it gets. Sheltered point breaks are perfect back-up spots on big swells, they filter the swell producing smaller and cleaner waves.

The bottom: Most point breaks have rocky bottoms, but they can also have sand, reef and boulder bottoms.

Currents: A local current usually follows the breaking wave direction down the point (known as a 'sweep', the opposite of a rip). To avoid it, paddle out from behind the peak at the top of the point, if there is a safe way to do so.

Famous point breaks: Rincon (California), Jeffrey's Bay (South Africa), Bells Beach (Australia).

DANGERS

The shore: Point breaks are harder to access than beachbreaks. The shore is usually covered with rocks and close to the breaking waves, complicating water entry and exit.
The bottom: Be wary of shallow rocks when falling. They can be sharp and covered with sea urchins.
Currents: At some point set ups, the current can be really strong and drag the unwitting surfer onto rocks or somewhere hard to get in or paddle back from.

✚ TIP

Local currents can be strong. To get back to the peak, walk along the beach instead of paddling if water exit and entry are easy.
Otherwise, paddle wide outside the waves to avoid the current.
In shallow waters, fall flat at the surface rather than penetrating deep.
If you need to step on the bottom, avoid kicking out in jerky movements. Smoothly test it before stepping on it.

REEF BREAK

At a reef break, waves break along a rock or coral reef following its shape. Their well-defined shape means swells move out of deep water to break suddenly with power on the shallow reef. Under the right conditions, reef breaks produce consistently hollow waves.

There are two types of coral reef breaks:

Barrier reef (reef pass): Usually surrounding volcanic islands, barrier reefs are separated from land by a lagoon. Gaps in the reef, known as passes are created by the effect of fresh water flowing off the land over time. The pass creates a corner in the reef over which peeling waves can break into a channel.
Fringing reef: Lining the shore, fringing reefs are usually created by a fossilized coral shelf, producing waves much closer to shore.

Reef waves generally break in the same spot, making for easier paddling out and positioning at the peak.
The main difficulties come from the wave itself, which breaks in shallow water really close to sharp coral, punishing any mistake by the surfer.
Advanced surfers love reef waves, because they are easy to read, powerful and at times close to perfection. Reef breaks offer the right shape and speed to make the best surfing moves, particularly the holy grail of surfing, tube riding.

Famous reef breaks: Cloudbreak (Fiji), Macaronis (Indonesia), Teahupoo (Tahiti), Pipeline (Hawaii).

DANGERS

Reef waves usually break over sharp, shallow coral.
Be aware of the water depth all along the wave before going for risky maneuvers.
Avoid the last 'closeout' maneuver in really shallow water. Contact with coral often means bloodshed, and cuts with a real risk of infection.

➕ TIP

Reef boots are the best way to protect feet when falling in shallow water. Adopt the 'starfish' strategy in a wipeout - falling as flat as possible, staying horizontal by spreading your arms and legs to avoid sinking deep. Without touching the bottom, use little, measured movements to get back to the surface. When going under waves, open your eyes to spot the reef and avoid contact.

UNDERSTANDING THE SPOT

O nce at the beach, the rush hits you. All you want to do is to wax your board, put your leash on and jump in. However, a few minutes taken to check the waves will often help you gain time and waves once in the surf zone. From the beach you can scan the entire spot, easily identifying its subtleties and dangers.

ANSWER THE RIGHT QUESTIONS

Check current direction and force: Observe water movements along the shoreline. Check if surfers are sitting or paddling constantly to maintain their position.

The bottom: Rock or sand? Note if waves break close to rocks or a jetty.

The waves: How are people surfing the spot? Are there surfers of your level?

Identify swell power and trends: The Internet forecast should reveal all. If not, count the interval between two waves. If it exceeds 12 seconds, you have a powerful long period swell that may well be building. Under 8 seconds, the swell will probably not rise significantly.

Tide: Get a tide book. If not, locate the high water mark on the beach, the upper limit of wet sand and debris. A wide wet beach below the high water mark means the tide is close to low. The same logic applies if large areas of seaweed or shellfish are visible on the rocks. At spots with large tidal ranges, be aware that a range of unseen hazards may present themselves as the tide moves both in and out.

PICK YOUR SPOT

Pick a marker on the beach in line with the peak you want to be surfing, particularly useful at beach breaks with currents and multiple peaks. Once in the surf, check it regularly to reposition yourself.

CHOOSE YOUR ENTRY PLAN

Locate the easiest way around the waves to reach the peak. The best option is to use the current to help you get there. For example, paddle out north of the peak if there is a southbound current.

MAKE AN EXIT PLAN

If exiting by rocks, jetty or reef exposed to waves, locate the safest way or 'key hole' before you go surfing.

CONDITION YOURSELF

From the beach, mind surf a couple of waves.

Visualize the way you want to surf them. Which lines? Which maneuvers?

JUMP IN

The paddle out usually gives you useful information to gain a feel for the spot from the inside.
You're now ready for a good session.
Have fun!

THE RULE OF 3

Evaluate wave size and allow 3 minutes of observation per foot :
3ft waves = 9 minutes observation before paddling out.
10ft waves = 30 minutes.
20ft waves = 1 hour.
Respect this rule in big surf, one error in judgment can bring heavy consequences.
(See 'Challenge and Commitment').

+ TIP

Get changed on the beach. This gives you extra time to observe the spot. Leaving your stuff in front of the wave you want to ride, you can keep an eye on it and use it as a fixed mark to position yourself.

CHOOSE YOUR WAVE

Y ou will never find two identical waves. At any spot during any session, you will get waves of all kinds: small, big, slow, fast, mushy, hollow, close-outs, shifty ones, as well as of course, the bombs. These unpredictable and random conditions, especially at beach breaks, require your permanent ability to observe and adapt. There is little use getting too exited and rushing to catch every wave that comes. Instead be proactive but selective, go for quality by observing and picking the right waves.

REDUCE MISTAKES

In the ever-changing ocean, wave selection will never be perfect, even for world champions. However, throughout your learning curve, you should aim to reduce mistakes in positioning and selecting waves.
Always assume there is a better wave to be had.
You will get little out of a wave too small, too fast or too weak.
But if you choose well, you should maximize your chances of getting enough wall and power to express yourself and accelerate your learning.

WAVE SELECTION BEGINS ON THE BEACH

Observing the spot carefully before each session helps you position yourself better and know which waves to surf.
Get into the rhythm: Locate where different waves break, the number per set and how they break.
Rank them in three categories:
- **The bombs:** These are the best waves to get, with the best surfing potential. Locate where they tend to break and pick a marker from the beach to help you find them once in the line-up.
- **The good ones:** These are not the best waves, but you can definitely ride them. These are the waves to be content with in crowded situations or conditions with long lulls.
- **The bad ones:** Too mushy, too short, too small or closing out, lacking the potential and energy for you to perform good maneuvers.

WAVE SELECTION CONTINUES IN THE WATER

Be in the right place: Once in the waves, monitor the horizon to see sets coming from far. This gives you enough time to anticipate their trajectory and position yourself.
Continue ranking the waves: As waves approach, try to read their potential in advance and make the right decision on whether or not to paddle.
Concentrate on the good ones and the bombs: Stop yourself from going for bad ones. They won't make you look good, but will make you waste time and energy.
Consider adjusting your marker: Note the positioning of other surfers, and pick a new marker on the beach if needed.

✚ TIP

If you loose your marker, let one good set go by and follow the white track left by the white water all the way to the peak.
If you have a hard time picking your waves and are only getting smaller ones, position yourself more on the outside. You'll be one step ahead for the bigger ones and will no longer be in a position to take the small ones.

ENERGY ZONES

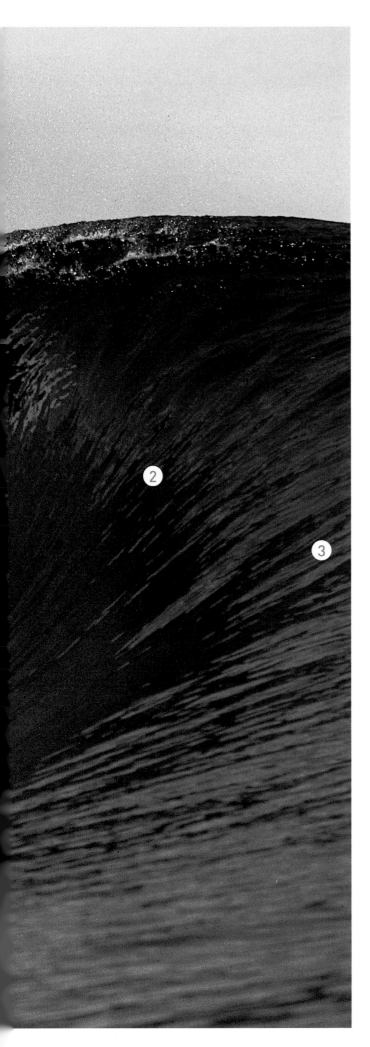

N othing beats the awesome spectacle of a breaking wave. Ever moving and unpredictable, the wave fascinates as much for its beauty as for the sensations it provides the surfer; varied sensations intimately related to its various energy zones.

1 The curl (or pocket): The maximum energy zone, where the wave stands vertical and breaks forward. It is here in the steepest and most hollow part of the wave that the surfer extracts maximum speed and experiences the strongest sensations. When breaking, the wave experiences an upward motion in the curl, helping the surfer go up the face.

2 The face: The medium energy zone, the 'blue' part of the wave, which stands but does not yet break forward. Less steep than the curl, the surfer gains stability on the face, but loses speed and potential for the best maneuvers.

3 The shoulder: The weak energy zone furthest from the curl, offering little energy or steepness to use. Lingering on the shoulder jeopardizes the rest of the ride.

4 The flats: The zone in front of the wave towards shore, where friction and a total lack of steepness rapidly slow the surfboard. Yet, it is a mandatory part of the transition for attacking the top of wave.

5 The lip: Above the curl, the lip is the 'white' part of the wave, which breaks or throws forward. A strong energy zone, but unstable, advanced surfers use it to accelerate during certain maneuvers.

6 The impact zone: Where the lip lands on the flats. Always avoid this zone whether surfing or paddling out, as the impact can be violent.

The foam or white water: The white part of the wave, which advances towards both the beach and the shoulder when waves break. Full of turbulence, it is hard to deal with, but can help the surfer get back into the wave when pushing his board against it.

The roll: Seen from underwater, the wave creates a circular motion which the surfer is directly in contact with when duck diving. Ahead of the roll, this circular motion, combined with turbulences created by the lip's impact pushes the surfer deeper underwater when duck diving. Behind the wave, the roll helps the surfer get back to the surface.

+ TIP

Go for a bodysurfing session. With swimming goggles, enjoy swimming in and around the waves to see all these zones and feel their different energies.

2.
USING THE WAVE'S ENERGY

The wave breaks the same for everybody.

Whether beginner or world champion, a wave makes no preference nor offers any privilege. The sole difference comes from your vision of the wave and what you want to do with it. In fact, the wave is like a mirror that reflects what you want to see and where you want to go.

TRAJECTORIES
HOW TO USE THE WAVE'S ENERGY

The trajectory or 'line' is the surfer's signature on the wave, the way he uses its energy and available space. It evolves according to each surfer's level and experience. There are 5 main types of line drawn through a surfer's progression.

These 5 steps show that progression in surfing is found by extending trajectories on the wave to cover the maximum of its available surfing space. The wave should always be the center of your attention.
Aim higher, lower, further and deeper!

1 | BEGINNER

The surfer is inactive in the white water and rides a straight line to the beach. He is using very little of the wave's energy and space.

+ TIP

Find a balanced and comfortable basic stance. Your back should be straight and relaxed, shoulder axis open towards the nose of the board. This correct basic stance will ease your progress, allowing optimum vision of the wave and making shoulder axis rotations much easier on both sides when you start doing turns. Avoid finding balance by bending your back over straight legs.

2 | PASSIVE SURFER

The surfer rides the wave's face passively sideways in a linear trajectory called 'trim line', which enables him to keep balance.
At this stage, the surfer uses the speed and energy provided by upward motion in the wave face. He uses more of the wave's energy and extends his trajectory over more of the wave.

+ TIP

After take-off, aim for the shoulder by applying pressure on the inside rail (rail in contact with the wave face). Once going sideways, release pressure on inside rail and apply to the outside (opposite) rail.

3 | SURFER GETTING ACTIVE

By getting active, the surfer generates his own speed. He goes up and down the wave and accelerates. He now uses more of the wave's height and extends his trajectory.

+ TIP

Try to extend this 's line' by going up and down the wave face. Use all your body height, applying (bending legs) and releasing pressure (extending legs) thinking, 'Small when bending, tall when releasing.'

4 | TOP-TO-BOTTOM SURFER

The surfer goes faster when he goes up and down using all of the available wave height in the curl, using the steepest slope that the wave offers. With this vertical, top-to-bottom trajectory, he constantly stays connected with the curl, accelerating and extending his line.

+ TIP

Aim for the very top and very bottom of the wave. Emphasize using your front foot when applying pressure on the rails in order to get to the limit of each slope.

5 | ADVANCED LEVEL SURFER

By maximizing his trajectory, the surfer gets maximum speed.
That speed gives him total freedom to exploit all of the wave's available space. He can go deep in the curl or away from it, he can use all of the wave's height and even use the space above it by executing innovative aerial maneuvers.
This is surfing of the highest level, as endorsed by the ASP judging criteria: Innovative and varied repertoire with speed, power and flow.

+ TIP

Try to go really fast. Vary your range of trajectories and maneuvers using all the space offered by the wave. Aim higher than the lip.

AIMING LOWER

Aiming at the bottom allows you to use all the wave's available height, gaining maximum speed and possibility for maneuvers. Each wave offers slopes to exploit. Under the effects of gravity, the more the surfer extends the descent, the more he accelerates. At the bottom, he has accumulated sufficient speed to use his rail to get back to the top to get a good maneuver in, and another new slope to use.

THE DANGER OF NOT DESCENDING ENOUGH

Turning too early before the bottom limits your speed and options – you have not created enough speed to get ahead of the wave – the wave follows you at its regular speed and catches you up. Too stuck in the face, you do not have enough speed and space to drive your board to the top. You have no choice but to go sideways to the shoulder.

Finding the bottom is a necessity if you want to do turns and keep gaining speed. When looking to accelerate down the wave face, you get ahead of it. You create sufficient speed and space to go into a strong bottom turn and choose the appropriate trajectory.

THE DANGER OF DESCENDING TOO MUCH

The steep slope ends in a gentle transition that becomes the flats, which do not give you anything. Friction forces are stronger on the flats and quickly slow your board.

FEEL AND TIMING

The bottom turn, depending on the surfer's speed at the end of the slope can take place more or less on the flats. The goal is to find the bottom, but certainly not lag there.

You need to feel when to stop going down and link into your bottom turn so that you can keep all the speed obtained going down.

✚ TIP

When getting to the bottom, try to make the most of your speed. Link your bottom turn spontaneously and immediately, just like the basketball bounces as soon as it hits the ground.

AIMING
HIGHER

AIMING FOR THE TOP MEANS GAINING

A NEW SLOPE TO USE

When aiming high on the wave, the double goal is to execute a nice maneuver, as well as to relaunch into the wave with maximum wave height to use.

The maximum wave height is always in the curl where the lip starts breaking.

Aiming as close to the lip as possible gives you the ideal slope to get speed, and the breaking lip will also push you back into the slope and help you accelerate.

CAUTION: Turning prematurely deprives you both of the lip's help and part of the wave height you could have used to descend into your next turn.

Make sure you wait until the nose of your board passes the lip before you start turning.

AIMING HIGHER SOMETIMES MEANS ABOVE THE LIP

A skateboarder accelerating up and down a ramp naturally ends up drawing higher vertical lines above the ramp. The same logic applies to surfing. As the surfer gets enough speed to keep going upwards, he can integrate aerial maneuvers into his repertoire.

In recent years, surfers have explored the aerial zone above the wave, creating diverse, complex and spectacular air moves.

+ TIP

Do you struggle to reach the top of the wave?
Aim above the lip, extending your bottom turn as if the wave were a foot bigger. If you keep looking above the lip and extending your body out of the bottom turn, you'll get there.

AIMING
FURTHER

AIMING FURTHER MAKES YOU EXTEND
YOUR SURFING PLAYGROUND

By gaining more and more speed, the surfer ends up going faster than the wave. This speed gives total freedom to get away from the curl to work with all the wave face towards the shoulder.

It's not about escaping from the curl, but getting temporarily away from it maintaining speed and drive, so that you can come back to it perfectly.

By aiming further, the surfer is not restricted only to vertical lines. He draws a full trajectory using all the wave's height and depth, drawing bigger lines and extending the surfable space on the wave.

CAUTION: This can be a risky line, because the shoulder provides little slope and energy. So as not to jeopardize your speed, feel and anticipate the moment you have to get back to the curl.

✚ TIP

Going further with a low line risks losing all your speed. Stay high so that you can use all available shoulder height to come back to the curl.

AIMING DEEPER

AIMING DEEPER MEANS SURFING MORE OF THE

WAVE AT THE PEAK

The goal is to extract maximum energy straight from take-off, intensifying your sensations.

When positioning and taking off behind the peak, the surfer immediately tucks in to the curl and uses its energy to make the section.
He feels the rush straight from take-off, in this, the maximum energy zone of the wave.

This kind of surfing on the edge forces the surfer to use his instincts, always ready to adapt and react immediately.

The most important thing is to dare to believe!
To progress, explore your limits. Taking new risks and exploring new zones will help your surfing evolve. When reaching your perceived limits, you realize you can always go one step further, the very act of progression.

✚ TIP

Avoid going straight down a fast-breaking wave from take-off, it would be like jumping off a moving train. Take a sideways angle straight from take-off so you can go with the down-the-line momentum. Benefit from paddling time to read the wave and choose the right trajectory. There is no room for hesitation - stick with your decision and go for it.

RIGHT PLACE
RIGHT TIME

Being in the right place at the right time is about choosing a trajectory adapted to how the wave is breaking.

FIND THE PERFECT LINE

The perfect line is the trajectory that allows for the best use of the wave's energy, so that you can maintain speed and flow through maneuvers.

Your priority is to stay continually connected to the wave's maximum energy zones by maneuvering your board through them.

Thus, your surfing gains amplitude, precision and beauty. You blend in with the flow of the wave with rhythm and fluidity.

READING THE WAVE

Reading the wave is essential. It allows you to see, feel and anticipate what the wave will do so that you can adapt to it instantaneously. It is the quality that separates excellent surfers from good surfers.

When paddling, reading the wave is mainly horizontal, to evaluate what it will do overall, to assess the speed and rhythm with which it will break.

Once up and riding, reading the wave also becomes vertical, so that you can use the entire slope to execute maneuvers. The goal is to keep a top-to-bottom trajectory close to the curl using all the slope available.

CAUTION: Reading a wave is never passive. It's done through action, and often requires last second trajectory adjustments to continually have the board in the right place.

✚ TIP

Build your surfing on good trajectories.
It is an absolute certainty that when you look for maximum energy zones, your flow and maneuvers get better.

3.

IN SYNERGY WITH THE WAVE

Tuning your energy to the wave.

The fundamentals of technique are your instruments. The wave dictates rhythm, tempo and key, the surfer must be in tune in order to play the right melody and make music. The art of the surfing is to harmonize fundamental movements in tune with the wave's rhythm.

WAVE VISION
ORIGIN OF
MOVEMENT

Your wave vision informs you of the wave's intentions. Always anticipating, your eyes are one step ahead of your actions. They analyze what's happening on the wave and help coordinate the movement in response.

When fixed on your next trajectory, your eyes lead to the rotation of your entire body. Eyes lead the shoulder axis, which drives the hips, which drive the legs, which drive the board.

Do not look at your feet, the fish or your friends on the shoulder. Look and aim at the furthest extension of your trajectory, because where your eyes go, your board will follow.

DO NOT MIX ANTICIPATION AND HASTE

If you look away from a zone too early, you'll never reach it. Keep your eyes fixed on the target until you are certain of reaching it. Then, start looking at the next zone you want to reach, and get there.
Timing is vital. Looking back to the top of the wave too early when beginning to drop down the face will make you go sideways and neglect your bottom turn, not properly using the steepness and not accelerating.

✚ TIP

When the eyes target, the body prepares.
Wave vision is the first thing to work on if you want to better your surfing. Be more ambitious. Keep visualizing the high and low parts of the wave, close to the curl, and feel instant results.
Again, we see the importance of trajectories. By focusing on the right trajectory, you're looking to the right zone on the wave, helping you keep accelerating and executing good maneuvers.

PUMP/RELEASE
THE BASIS OF SPEED

This core action is fundamental to your progression as a surfer. When pumping your surfboard by bending your legs, the rail goes underwater, and in reaction, your board wants to pop out due to forces of buoyancy. The surfer creates an acceleration due to the buoyancy effect and flex of the surfboard - the more you compress your board underwater by applying strong and steady pressure, the more it lifts when you release. Downward pressure should be released when your board is aiming at the zone you are targeting. The idea is to totally release pressure by extending and projecting your body towards your next target. Released of pressure, your rail pops out and frees all the energy accumulated during compression – you are creating your own speed. Your board then upthrusts or 'drives' straight into the next turn.

FINDING DRIVE

Many surfers pump to instigate the buoyancy upthrust, but do not extend their body enough to fully release it. The release is as important as the compression itself, not only does it facilitate your acceleration, but it also helps you reload power so you can compress into the next turn better.
In between turns, take the opportunity to extend your body and let the board accelerate, while you get 'reloaded'.

THE WAVE DECIDES

You can't apply the same pressure in terms of length and intensity all the time. It depends on the wave size and power, and the zone you want to reach. E.g. Too short at the bottom turn, the pressure created will not generate enough drive to take you to the top.

WHEN?

Use this action any time you want to gain speed, when looking to accelerate horizontally down the line, or when doing top and bottom turns.

✚ TIP

Think of your body as a spring, the more it bends and compresses the board, the more it can extend, allowing the board to accelerate towards your next target.

THE SHOULDER AXIS
DIRECTION AND AMPLITUDE
OF MOVEMENT

Shoulder axis rotation is the action that helps steer your board into and through your next move up or down the wave. Throughout a turn, your shoulders should rotate and point towards the next target. As the shoulder axis rotates, it leads the rest of your body and ultimately the board. To maximize this rotation, keep your torso straight and relaxed.

IMPORTANCE OF ABDOMINAL CORE STRENGTH

Contracting your abdominal muscles helps you keep control with maximum energy.
If your upper and lower body are not linked through rotation, the energy of your movement is not contained and gets scattered, which reduces the amplitude of your turns and your speed.
Contracting your core muscles conserves the energy generated by upper body rotation and transmits it to your legs, allowing you to keep pressure on rails, draw longer lines and accelerate.

ROTATION / COUNTER-ROTATION

As you rotate around the shoulder axis, you are also preparing your next turn, accumulating energy and amplitude to be released when you decide.
Think of it like a rubber band - the more you pull it one way, the more it will go back the other.
Your goal is to use maximum rotation for maximum effect.
E.G. Out of your bottom turn, 'stretch the rubber band' by fully rotating your shoulder axis towards the top of the wave. As you reach the top, release it into a counter-rotation in the opposite direction, driving your top turn and flowing into the next move.

TIMING

Rotation and counter-rotation have to be timed and tuned into the wave, so that they give full power and speed to your turns. Timing your rotations properly means you control where you go on the wave, and when.
Rotating too early:
When you use all your available shoulder rotation too soon, you are forced to counter-rotate, which immediately stops the climb.
Not rotating fully:
A half rotation means a half turn. You also miss the opportunity to optimise the drive and power of your next turn.

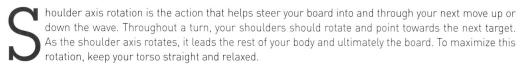

Refine your basic stance, the one you have from take-off, in the tube and in between turns. Open your shoulder axis towards the nose of the board, avoid it being parallel to the stringer.
When your upper body leads the direction of your trajectory, you gain potential for rotation, time and vision. You can read and react better to the wave.
Breathing: Synchronize muscle contractions and breathing phases, so that you inhale, relax and extend between turns, letting your board flow and recharging your batteries before you compress and exhale during the turn.

THE ARMS

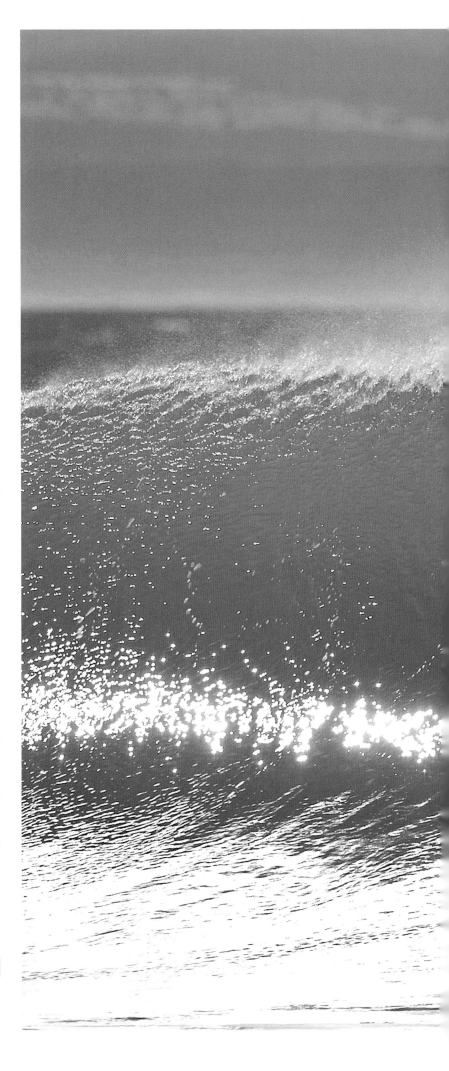

As the extremities of your upper body, your arm positions and movements help you flow and balance as you surf. Your arms play a variety of roles that you need to identify and understand to gain optimum control.

STABILIZING ROLE

The wave, in constant multi-directional movement destabilizes your balance. You must permanently compensate to maintain balance and the right trajectory. Dangling by your sides, your arms offer little. They are more helpful raised chest-high and ready to react to any change.

DIRECTIONAL ROLE

The arms play a part in steering your line.
Positioned forward, they lead you ahead. They should aim for your next turn, especially the front arm, which is always anticipating the direction of your trajectory.

AMPLIFYING ROLE

Rotation amplifier:
Your arms are the extension of your shoulder axis. If they are 'locked' to the shoulders, they help increase rotation and thus the quality of your turns.

Heaviness / lightness:
Lowering your arms close to your body amplifies pressure on the board through turns. Raising your arms encourages lightness to emphasize the rebound effect from the turn.
E.g. Raising your arms out of the bottom turn eases and quickens your climb up the face.

SENSITIVE ROLE

Touching the water helps you gain information - you can feel your speed and know exactly where you are on the wave.

+ TIP

Touching the wave face when turning means you are fully leaning on and burying the rail, as well as providing a center point to rotate around.

FRONT & BACK FOOT SURFING

Your feet are the extension of your body and your contact with the board. Both the front and back foot have specific roles depending on the situation.

OFF THE FRONT FOOT

Board flat: Getting your weight on the front foot makes your board plane and fit the slope as you descend the wave. It allows water release through the tail with less resistance, therefore amplifying down slope speed. (Taking-off, exiting turns.)

Board on rail: Weighting your front foot allows you to use the entire rail through turns. You want the maximum length of rail underwater to get maximum drive in phases where you look to amplify your turns. (Bottom turning, cutting back, carving.)

OFF THE BACK FOOT

Quick change of direction: To turn quickly in a short space, back foot pressure is applied when you want to get radical on your top turns, or to get vertical exiting your bottom turn or cutback.

Stalling: Lifting the nose out of the water to suddenly slow down, i.e. when looking for the tube is done by heavily weighting the back foot.

Generating 'pop': The back foot is first weighted before then releasing the tail in all versions of tail slides and aerials (see Maneuvers chapter). Brief back foot pressure puts the tail underwater before its release induces it to pop out.

HEELS SIDE PRESSURE

To turn on heels side rail.

TOES SIDE PRESSURE

To turn on toes side rail .

✚ TIP

Identify your dominant foot (the one you tend to favor when going down the line). Fully release off your back foot between turns, keeping it weighted too long slows the board. Weight your front foot to flow and extend your lines.

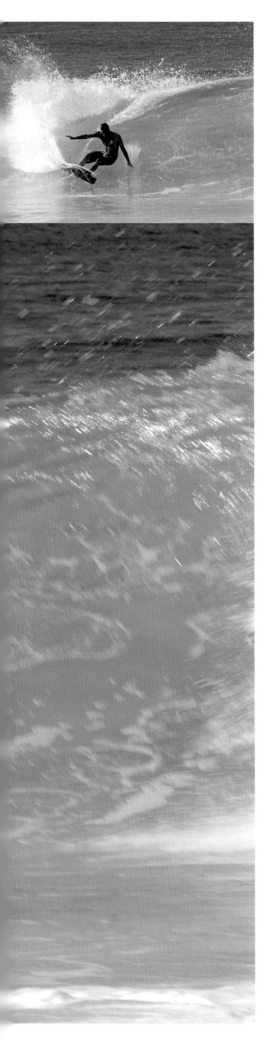

HIPS AND
WEIGHT SHIFTS

Shifting your weight forwards and backwards has a major influence on wave usage, and allows a compromise between the need for speed and the desire to make radical turns. When shifting your weight backwards you can make tight radius, radical turns. Then shift it forward to gain speed out of a turn and flow to the next one. Modern shortboards do not allow walking along the board to shift your weight, instead your hips play this role. When mobile, your hips amplify weight shifts. For example, when exiting the bottom turn, a forward hip movement coordinated with the body extension will generate speed.

SHIFTING WEIGHT FORWARDS

Down slope: Bring your knees in along the stringer, opening hips and shoulders towards the nose.

Out of the bottom turn: Totally extend your body to the top, moving hips forward to facilitate drive. Turning your shoulder axis towards the target amplifies this weight shift.

SHIFTING WEIGHT BACKWARDS

Take your back knee outside the board, closing hips and shoulder axis.
This helps tighten your turns to go vertical.

NOTE: Scared of falling, many surfers limit their movements and weight shifts along the board, thus limiting their repertoire and skills. On the other hand, the best surfers master the art of weight shifting, loading and unloading to optimize their board's contact with the wave. The board 'flies' and the surfer gives an impression of mastery, flow and grace.

✚ TIP

Practice out of the water:
On a longboard skateboard, start drawing lines on a gentle slope. Try different positions by moving hips and knees forward. Note their impact on your amplitude and speed though the lines.

Feel it in the water:
Move your hips along the stringer to shift weight to the front. To amplify your lines, complement this movement with shoulder rotations.

SURFING IN TUNE

TIMING

In order to surf in tune and in time, you must feel the wave's rhythm and blend in. Your ride is a chain of actions, and how you link those actions is vital to your flow on the wave.
The perfect ride is when you fit in key actions in harmonious flow with an ideal trajectory.

OPTIMIZE PADDLING

Paddle hard enough to catch up with the wave. Always give an extra stroke before take-off, the goal being to gain time and momentum into the down slope.

GET AHEAD OF THE WAVE

Focus on a quick wave entry by keeping your weight forward. This is no time to be passive - accelerate and get ahead of the slope.

CHOOSE THE RIGHT TRAJECTORY

You first trajectory is dictated by the wave's speed.

Slow wave: Choose a vertical trajectory so that you can keep in contact with the steepest slope of the curl and accelerate.

Fast wave: Straight from take-off, your goal is to get one step ahead of the wave by driving directly towards the shoulder. This quick rail pump, followed by a total release and extension should give you enough speed and projection to get your board up the face. Matching the wave's rhythm, you're ready to use a new slope with more momentum.

REACH THE BOTTOM

Certain fast breaking waves might require more than one high line pump. Do as many as you need, but do not forget to then plant a good bottom turn, the basis of all good top turns. Once you have gained enough speed high on the face, descend all the way down using this speed and the slope to crank a solid bottom turn, which will set you up for the best trajectory.

MAINTAIN SPEED

Between turns
Going downhill on a bike, instinct tells you to stop pedaling. The cyclist takes this moment to relax

and recover as the bike goes alone under gravity. Conversely, he must pedal hard to go uphill.
To keep speed, it is important to understand how the wave slope works differently.
- Getting ahead of the wave by going down means fully using the slope, one of your rare opportunities to naturally accelerate. The steeper the wave is, the more you have to compensate with balance and feel to maintain both speed and control. Keep active, shifting your weight forward in order to reach the bottom and have full potential for maneuvers.
- Use the wave's energy to go back up. When going up the face, the wave advances towards you, naturally helping you climb. After a good compression at the bottom turn, make yourself as light and relaxed as possible, standing up straight and raising your arms, so that the board lifts and climbs. This relaxed state aids your flow and recovers the power you'll need for your top turn.

During turns
Using the slope alone does not necessarily mean keeping your speed through turns. Once at the bottom or top, avoid losing precious time passively observing the next zone - thinking without acting kills your speed. **Anticipate, react.**
Like a ball bouncing as soon as it hits the ground, be ready to link your maneuvers as you reach the top and bottom, so you can be on rail and using all the energy without waste.
Without waiting for a perfect response from the wave, get on rail and rebound immediately and spontaneously. Then adjust your trajectory to your next target as you go.

FUNCTIONAL MANEUVERS

Choose each maneuver so you can adapt it to the wave and use it to accelerate to the next one.
Push through the whole move and only release when you know the board is accelerating into the next turn. Then relax and let the board flow until your next compression.
Alternating compression and release is fundamental to good surfing. Think of it like breathing in and out.

✛ TIP

Learning these different techniques can only be done at the appropriate stages on a wave. Spend as much time as you need to feel out how each one applies, starting with the one that facilitates the rest of your ride - the wave entry.

CORRECTING
YOUR LINE

To go faster and do better turns, your goal is to find the right trajectory while fitting in the best moves. Diagnose and adjust your line by recognizing your typical trajectory.

HORIZONTAL SURFING

Symptoms: The surfer tends to ride sideways to the shoulder. He is stuck to the wave, only using its upper part. He can go fast, but his movements and maneuvers lack amplitude.
Treatment: Use a thicker board. For a few sessions, focus solely on the bottom turn until you have it right and can add it to your repertoire.
Trajectory: Gain speed, then break your line by pointing your board vertically down the wave, in order to have both the momentum and the angle for a legitimate driving bottom turn.
Technique: For better speed and control down the face, shift your weight over the front foot, opening your shoulder axis towards the bottom. Once at the bottom, start pushing hard while your board is pointing at the beach.

'V' SURFING

Symptoms: The surfer chooses good trajectories but gets stuck though each turn. He pivots his board on the tail instead of driving off his rails.
Treatment: Use more front foot, and the full length of the rails through turns.
Trajectory: Draw more rounded and fuller turns, to get a 'capital U' line.
Technique: Use more front foot through turns and rotate the shoulder axis to extend and hold the line.

'W' SURFING

Symptoms: The surfer loses speed at the bottom where he tends to do two or more brief and useless pumps. He loses all his momentum and cannot properly drive off the bottom.
Treatment: Avoid multiple short pumps off the bottom in favor of one, driving bottom turn.
Trajectory: Draw one, full 'capital U' line.
Technique: Drive cleanly off the bottom by keeping constant pressure on your inside rail through the 'U'.

SMALL 'U' SURFING

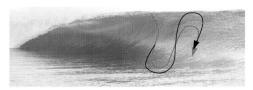

Symptoms: The surfer finds the bottom and links bottom turns, but struggles to reach the top.
Treatment: Apply rail pressure fully until the target, using all the wave's height.
Trajectory: Draw a 'capital U' line by extending your bottom turn to the top.
Technique: Keep driving the rail off the bottom by aiming higher than the lip. Work on increasing drive by delaying your body extension slightly.

'J' SURFING

Symptoms: The surfer knows how to use his rails, but loses too much time at the bottom of the wave. He is not spontaneous, reacting too late instead of anticipating. He loses speed and opportunity for maneuvers.

Treatment: Start pushing off the bottom earlier, just before reaching the bottom.

Trajectory: Draw a vertical line straight down to the flats.

Technique: Apply pressure on the rail earlier, just before reaching the flats, at the top of the 'U'. Then hold pressure through the whole turn by delaying your body extension slightly.

OPEN 'U' SURFING

Symptoms: The surfer knows how to use his rails but never gets vertical. He rides the blue parts of the wave but never attacks the white zones. He is not targeting correctly.

Treatment: Go more vertical, straight up and straight down the face.

Trajectory: Draw more vertical lines with tighter angles.

Technique: Keep on the back foot and increase shoulder rotation when completing your bottom turns. As you come off the bottom, keep your eyes on the lip until you are sure to reach it.

When top turning, hold the turn until your board is aiming down the wave.

Pump
····· Release

+ TIP

Get someone to video you.

First watch your rides focusing only on your trajectories.

Then watch them again, focusing on your technique and timing. Be critical and correct yourself.

········· symptom
———— treatment

4.
THE
SURFBOARD

The surfboard is your physical bond with the wave, and your medium for expressing yourself.

Like a brush to a painter, or an instrument to a musician, the surfboard must be forgotten and become an extension of you. Rather than an object, it is a vehicle for generating sensations. There are an endless variety of surfing playgrounds. To have fun and to best experience all of them, you must also vary your surfboard.

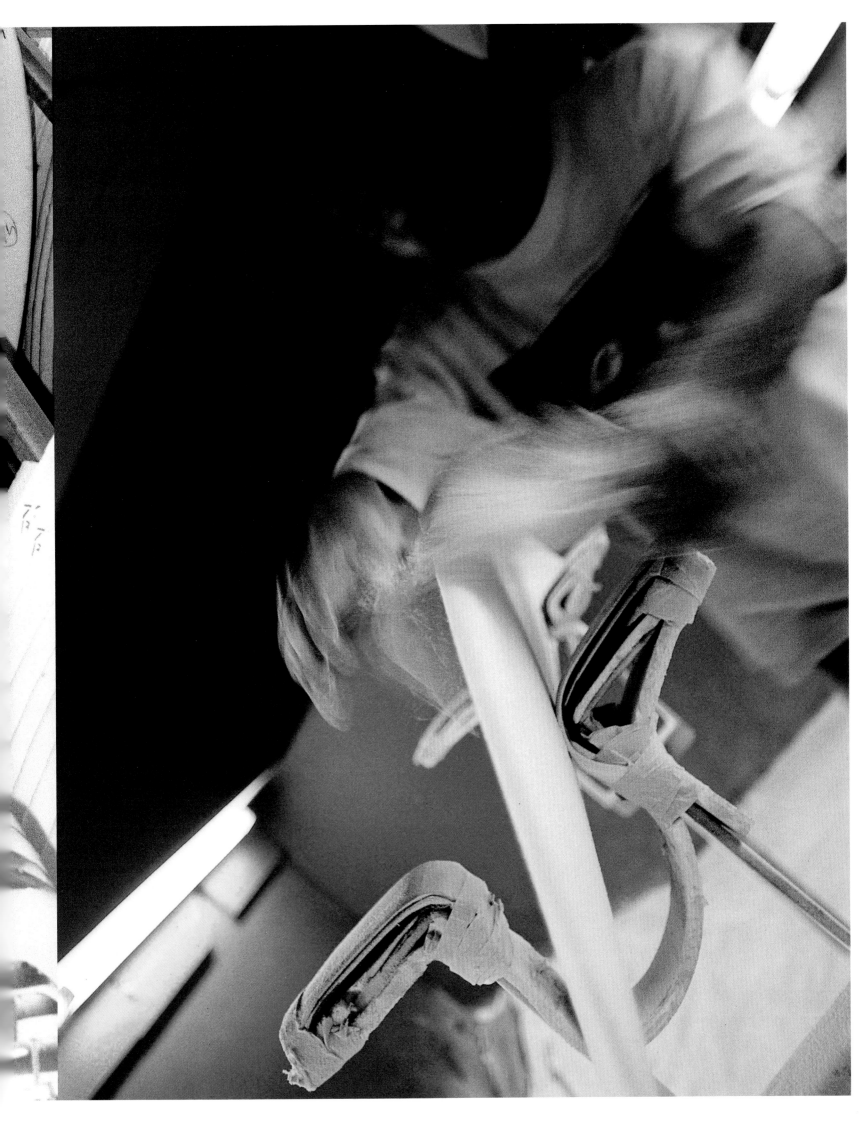

SQUASH

SQUARE

ROUND

DIAMOND

BABY SQUASH

ROUNDED PIN

SWALLOW

PINTAIL

BABY SWALLOW

SURFBOARD PARAMETERS

OUTLINE (OR PLANSHAPE)

The general shape of the board, as seen from above or below. Different outlines are associated with different design types, such as longboard, shortboard, gun, funshape, fish, etc....

LENGTH

Usually relates to wave size. The bigger the surf, the longer the board, allowing the surfer to catch waves and surf with control. In smaller surf, boards get shorter to surf closer to the curl and perform tighter turns.

WIDTH

Affects buoyancy, speed and control during turns. Boards are generally wider for small weak waves, narrower in bigger, hollower surf.

THICKNESS

Along with width, thickness governs the overall 'volume' and thus buoyancy of the board. Thicker boards increase stability, paddling speed and drive, but decrease maneuverability. Thus a compromise must be found relating to the surfer's weight and ability for a thickness that gives paddling and wave catching ease but also allows for maneuvers.

RAILS

The board's contact with the wave through turns. Rounded or 'boxy' rails are forgiving but sacrifice ease of turning. Pinched or 'low' rails make the board more reactive. Thicker rails are useful in weak waves to float and drive. In designs for powerful, hollow waves, rail thickness is reduced to help grip the face and give control through high speed turns.

TAIL

The 'business end' of the board, with a big influence on maneuvers. Wide and angled tails are fast and loose and suited to small waves, where they want to pop out of turns and fly over flat sections. Pointed, narrower tails tend to sink but ease rail to rail transitions. Ideal for steep, hollow waves where they give grip and control.

BOTTOM

Concaves: curves shaped into the bottom of the board from rail to rail viewed at cross section. Either single, double or a combination of both give the board speed and maneuverability by channeling water to the fins quicker, and provide drive through turns by lowering rails relative to the stringer.
Vee: when the stringer is lower than the rails. Facilitates rail to rail transitions, but makes the board less responsive than concaves.
Modern surfboards can mix both concave and vee to benefit from both.

FINS

Give drive and grip to the board, allowing it to turn without sideslipping or 'spinning out'. The most popular fin set-up remains the tri-fin, or thruster, with two side fins close to the rails and a rear fin in the middle to control and extend turns. Generally, the heavier and more powerful the surfer, the more fin surface he prefers.

ROCKER

The bottom curve of the board from nose to tail. Generally flatter in small wave designs to generate speed, more pronounced in powerful waves to optimize control and maneuverability.

Nose rocker: The curve at the nose, which eases wave entry in steep waves and facilitates turns.
Tail rocker: The curve or lift in the tail, which allows for water release and increased maneuverability.
Middle curve: Flattest and fastest part of the rocker which the surfer uses to maintain speed in between turns or inside the tube.

1. Small waves:
squash, square, round
2. Intermediate waves:
diamond, baby squash, rounded pin
3. Hollow, powerful waves:
pin tail, baby swallow

CHOOSING
THE RIGHT BOARD

Surfing is a connection between you and the wave, made possible by the surfboard. To make this connection a success, your board must be adapted to:
- Your build.
- Your ability.
- The waves you want to surf.

BEGINNER'S BOARD:

FINDING YOUR BALANCE

The beginner generally does not generate his own speed. To ride waves, he relies on the wave's speed and the stability of his board.
At this stage, look for stability and volume to aid paddling, wave catching and balance.

Opt for a board:
- At least 10" longer than you are tall.
- At least 20" wide.
- At least 2 ¾" thick.
Over-sizing your dimensions provides paddling comfort and easier wave entry. On the wave, the board provides enough stability and cruising speed, allowing you to develop a relaxed and balanced basic stance.

CAUTION: Do not get ahead of yourself. Starting with too small a board often leads to bad habits in technique, which will ultimately slow your progress.

INTERMEDIATE'S BOARD:

EXPLORING THE WAVE

Comfortable on your feet and well balanced, you can start to think about the wave itself. As you become more active, you can explore new zones with new priorities, not only looking for a board with stability, but also with maneuverability.
It's time to tune your surfboard.
Reduce length: To get vertical and radical, even in the powerful zones of the wave.

Reduce width: To favor rail to rail surfing.
Reduce thickness: To use your rails better and make radical turns.

FINDING THE 'MAGIC' SURFBOARD

As you progress and surf more in the curl, you can tweak your surfboard dimensions, chiefly by reducing them in to get more radical. Just be careful not to sacrifice speed and flow for turning ability. Find the right balance to keep enough speed and buoyancy and develop your style.

BUILDING YOUR QUIVER

Part of your path to being a complete surfer is exploring different playgrounds and making the most out of different conditions. In this quest, you'll need a multi-purpose quiver:
The 'flyer': Small wave board, short, wide and thick. Should have enough volume and buoyancy to support you and fly through weak conditions, typical of summer surf.
The 'all-round': The board to surf in all conditions between three to eight feet surf. Relatively short but thinner than the flyer, to be able to surf critical sections and make radical turns in more powerful waves.
The 'step-up': A longer board, thicker in the middle, but narrow and thin in the nose and tail to maintain control in bigger, powerful surf.

GOLDEN RULE
Whatever the conditions, opt for too much surfboard over not enough. Extra volume means faster paddling, easier wave entry, more speed and better linkage.

+ TIP

Consult your shaper. He will help you find the magic board and put together a quiver adapted to your playgrounds.

5.
MANEUVERS

Each maneuver has a specific function to fit the wave.

Each maneuver should be considered not in isolation, but as a means to maintaining speed and transitioning into the next. Maneuvers ill-timed or executed in the wrong part of the wave can compromise the rest of your ride. This does not mean you cannot be creative or should be conservative. You just need to remember that the best maneuvers are always the result of a good trajectory. Understanding the various maneuvers and knowing when to perform them will give spontaneity to your surfing and allow you to quickly develop a varied repertoire.

PADDLING

THE VAST MAJORITY
OF THE TIME YOU SPEND IN THE
WATER SURFING WILL BE TIME
SPENT PADDLING YOUR BOARD.
PADDLING IS OF PARAMOUNT
IMPORTANCE SINCE IT IS HOW
YOU GET INTO THE LINEUP,
AND HOW YOU CATCH WAVES
ONCE YOU ARE THERE.

PADDLING

In any sport, good technique leads to efficiency and economy of movement. In the case of paddling, good technique saves energy for longer sessions, as well as giving you optimum freedom of movement in the surf, at times allowing you to avoid danger.

POSITION

Lying on your board, distribute your weight evenly so that it can glide over the water. It should sit on the surface of the water at the same angle it would float if you weren't lying on it, neither pointing up nor down.

Weighted too far forwards the board nose dives, too far back it shoves water and slows down. Adjust your position until you feel the best flow.

Your entire body should be prone and in contact from legs to ribs, except your upper torso and head which is raised to favor paddling and vision.

Stay centered: Contract your abdominals and keep your legs straight and close together. Your head should stay on course, not turning side to side with each paddling stroke.

ARM MOVEMENT

Alternately, each arm reaches out as far ahead as possible before going underwater.

Your hand does the work: Your fingers, straightened and spread slightly should shovel underwater, pulling you ahead with each stroke. Fill your hand with water before pulling.

Make sure you keep your arms straight and parallel to the rail all along the stroke underwater.

Avoid finishing the movement too far back, instead pull each arm out of the water as you reach your hips. Then bend it, elbow up, so you can extend it ahead for your next stroke smoothly.

Relax neck and shoulders to gain maximum amplitude of stroke.

RHYTHM

Cruising: To move around in the surf zone, find a cruising speed using moderate, regular movements, not too fast or forced. The goal is to move around without wearing yourself out.

Sprinting: Your paddling pace should accelerate in certain situations- to catch the wave, when duck diving to help create momentum to sink the board and when caught inside trying to get under the wave before it breaks.

In these situations, you need a burst of paddling speed, but your movement should stay coordinated and efficient to avoid wasting energy and getting out of breath.

+ TIP

When pressing your chest to the board, your arm reaches further ahead and under. As you pull your arm out, raise your chest slightly, lightening you and helping you accelerate. Try this variation in chest height when you want to paddle fast, particularly for the last strokes before take-off.

DUCK DIVING

AT CERTAIN TIMES IT IS
IMPOSSIBLE TO PADDLE
AROUND THE BREAKING
WAVES, INSTEAD YOU MUST
PADDLE THROUGH THEM.
IN ORDER TO REACH THE
LINEUP, YOU NEED TO DUCK
DIVE.
DUCK DIVING ALLOWS YOU TO
GO THROUGH THE SURF ZONE
BY PASSING UNDERNEATH
WAVES AS THEY BREAK AND
ROLL TOWARDS SHORE.

DUCK DIVING

Duck diving requires passing underneath breaking waves as you paddle out. As it breaks the wave creates turbulence, which you avoid by sinking your board underneath it. Your goal is to avoid getting swept backwards. The better you duck dive, the faster you will reach the peak and take your next wave.

Create momentum
As the wave approaches, accelerate your paddling pace, you need momentum to help sink the board.

1. Sink the board
Gripping both rails, extend your arms down, sinking the nose of the board with all your weight, at an angle of 45° to the surface.
Timing: Sink the board at the last instant, the wave less than ten feet away, because your buoyancy will quickly make you pop back to the surface. With good timing, you can use the buoyancy to surface behind the wave. Executed too early, you'll pop up directly into the turbulent zone.

2. Use the wave
Underwater, waves make a circular motion with strong turbulence under the lip's impact, and an upward motion behind it. This turbulence can destabilize you, but if deep enough, it can help you sink your board. Then, as the wave passes, you benefit from the circular movement to surface on the other side.
CAUTION: You can never totally avoid the turbulence. Stay alert and grip your rails tight to keep hold of your board.

3. Orientation
Key to your duck dive is sinking the board at 45° to the surface at the exact moment the turbulence passes over. Then, firmly press on the tail with your foot or knee, so that it sinks deeper than the nose. As the water passes over in a circular motion, lead the upthrust at 45° to the surface by looking up.
CAUTION: If your nose is deeper than your tail at this moment, the wave will carry you backwards and your duck dive is ineffective.

➕ TIP

Open your eyes underwater. You'll realize the turbulences are uneven, with some deeper and more intense than others.
Aim your board towards the weaker ones or try to 'hide' in between two pockets.
To surface quicker, tilt your board on one rail.

© Jon Frank

TAKING OFF

THE TAKE-OFF IS THE VERY
BEGINNING OF YOUR RIDE,
PREPARING FOR EACH
STEP THAT FOLLOWS.
WELL EXECUTED, IT ALLOWS
YOU TO GAIN SPEED INTO THE
WAVE AND LINK MANEUVERS.
SLOW AND PASSIVE, IT GETS
YOU STUCK, CONDEMNING
YOU TO FALLING
OR MISSING THE RIDE.
CONTRARY TO POPULAR
BELIEF, EACH AND EVERY
WAVE ENTRY IS IMPROVABLE,
FROM BEGINNER TO EXPERT.

TAKE-OFF: WAVE ENTRY

Two distinct phases make up a good wave entry: Paddling acceleration, and jumping to your feet.

PADDLING

Before take-off, paddling helps create enough speed to catch the wave.

Launching phase: Be aware of the timing of your paddling acceleration. Don't paddle like crazy for a whole minute before the wave arrives. While it is still approaching, your goal is to gain a steady pace to position yourself.

Final sprint: When the wave is less than 12 feet away, give your maximum effort, paddling hard and fast to catch the wave.

CAUTION: Sprinting too early will cause you to waste the energy needed to get into the wave before it reaches you. On the other hand, sprinting too late does not create enough speed. In both cases, you miss the wave.

STANDING UP

Leap up on your board: As you feel the wave lift your tail and carry you, push on both arms and jump to your feet. This should be a rapid, one-step jump.
Deploy the rest of your body:
Once on your feet, smoothly deploy your upper body

into your surfing stance. Avoid transferring your weight to the back foot, rather keep it on the front foot, aiding acceleration down the slope.
Once accelerating down, straighten your upper body to prepare your bottom turn.

Function:
Launch into the wave as fast and as early as possible.
Goal:
To take maximum speed from the slope, gaining time and space for a good bottom turn.
Trajectory:
Look for a vertical line to the bottom, with your board fitting the slope.
Technique:
Keep low, with back bent over front foot to make the board fit the slope and accelerate.
Try:
Before standing up, give a final extra paddling stroke with your chin and chest low to your board, to give initial momentum down the slope.
Avoid:
Standing up too early, which can cause unwanted weight transfer to tail. In the worst-case scenario, especially in hollow waves, you'll lose speed instantaneously, and risk getting stuck in the lip.

HOLLOW WAVE TECHNIQUE:
Angle your take-off to grip the face and avoid falling. Before standing up, retract your inside arm slightly to predispose opening the shoulders towards that rail, engaging it in the face.

➕ TIP

Go to all the extremes to note the impact of your weight on the board. Stand up straight immediately on the back of the board and feel how this slows you. Then try taking-off keeping your back bent forward down the slope. You'll realize a bent upper body helps you accelerate, and that the hollower the waves are, the more you need to keep your weight forward when taking off.

BOTTOM TURN

THE BOTTOM TURN IS FUNDAMENTAL TO YOUR RIDE. YOU NEED IT TO FOLLOW THE WAVE'S TRAJECTORY, SETTING YOU UP FOR A WIDE RANGE OF MANEUVERS. A COMMON MISTAKE IS TO FOCUS ONLY ON TOP TURNS, NEGLECTING THE BOTTOM TURN THAT FACILITATES THEM. THE TRUTH IS, WITHOUT A GOOD BOTTOM TURN THERE WILL BE NO GOOD TOP TURN. A GOOD BOTTOM TURN IS VITAL IF YOU WANT TO IMPROVE AND DEVELOP YOUR SURFING.

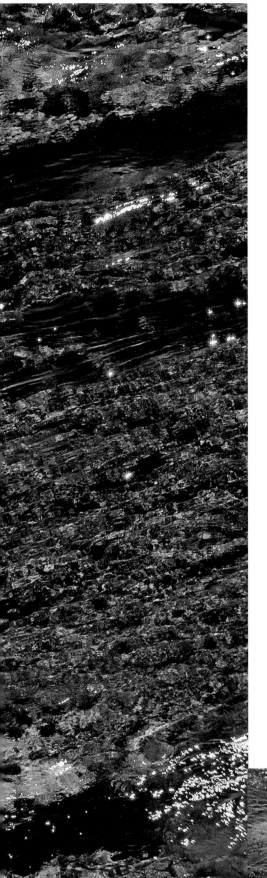

FOREHAND BOTTOM TURN

In all types of waves, the bottom turn is a prerequisite for all top turns. It should be your main focus before your start going for radical top turns. It can be squared off the bottom to go vertical if you have time, or extended to the shoulder in faster breaking waves to cover more ground. A good bottom turn should maintain or amplify the speed obtained through the drop, and lead you to the best zone of the wave.

1. Timing
As when you reach the flats you start losing speed. Seize the opportunity to rebound immediately so you can keep all the speed accumulated in going down face.
Bend both legs, with weight and pressure evenly distributed along the rail, and lean on your inside (toe side) rail.

2. One constant pressure
Applying sufficient pressure on your rail gives drive, which makes you turn with speed and power.
Take full advantage of this energy by keeping your rail engaged until you are aiming at your target.

3. Total extension
Once aiming at the target, release your rail by totally extending your body. Timed and executed correctly, your board will accelerate to the top.

Targeting
Focus on the target. Targeting close to the lip will not only offer you a strong maneuver, but also an ideal position from which to take a steep line into your next bottom turn.

Function:
Rebound from wave base with maximum speed.
Goal:
To use maximum speed from the drop to project up to the top of the wave.
Trajectory:
Draw a tight 'U' line to stay vertical and close to the pocket.
Technique:
Keep constant rail pressure throughout the 'U', your body compact, strong and over the maximum rail length.
Try:
Touching the wave as far away as possible from your board with your inside (trailing) hand, to ensure you're leaning into the turn and using your rail. Use it as a center point of rotation to draw your 'U' around until it is time to extend.
Avoid:
Lagging in the flats, where all your speed will be lost. Also avoid multiple pump bottom turns, which kill your speed.

+ TIP

Start the bottom turn with your shoulder line opened towards the nose of your board. It will then have to rotate fully through the 'U' and help you drive your bottom turn.

2

1

3

BACKHAND BOTTOM TURN

The backhand bottom turn involves the same principles as the forehand bottom turn. It needs a good steep line in to use maximum wave steepness, and good leg compression to keep speed throughout the turn. You also have an advantage on your backhand - rail compression is easier on your heel side.

1. Aim the board towards the beach
Aim your board vertically down the wave face to accelerate. When reaching the flats, immediately go into the bottom turn.

2. Lean
When going fast on a bike, you have to lean to be able to turn sharply. On a surfboard the same principal applies. Lean back on your heals to start turning and direct your line.
If possible, touch the water with your leading hand: you gain a valuable pivot point to turn around.
The more powerful the wave, the more you will have to dig in and lean over the rail.

3. Look above your shoulder
As your board starts accelerating though the turn, look over your shoulder targeting the lip. Focusing on the lip keeps your turn fast and tight. Keep low with a hand in the water until your board is aiming at the very top of the wave.

Total extension
Spring out of the compressed bottom turn when your board is aimed at the right zone. Use this total extension to then complete your shoulder rotation, placing your board in the target zone you want to reach.
This tight rotation will then set up a good wave position from which to execute your top turn and flow into the next section.

Function:
Rebound from wave base with maximum speed.
Goal:
Use maximum speed from the drop to project up to the top of the wave.
Trajectory:
Draw a tight 'U' line to stay vertical and close to the pocket.
Technique:
Start the bottom turn with your shoulder axis closed, parallel to the stringer.
Try:
Touching the wave as far away as possible from your board with your inside (leading) hand, to ensure you're leaning into the turn and using your rail. Use it as a center point of rotation to draw your 'U' around until it is time to extend.
Avoid:
A common mistake on your backhand is to turn your shoulders too early, in order to have a better view of the wave. If you open your shoulders too soon, your body extends, loses power and reduces the rail compression needed for acceleration.

✚ TIP

Use a full shoulder rotation to get to the lip, holding the rotation until you pass mid-face to gain maximum drive. Your back shoulder is like an 'eye' - it should 'see' your target before you reach the top of the wave.

OFF THE LIP

THE OFF THE LIP/RE-ENTRY IS THE NATURAL OUTCOME OF YOUR BOTTOM TURN. IT IS A RADICAL TURN THAT WILL ALSO HELP YOU RE-LAUNCH INTO THE SLOPE. GOOD OFF THE LIPS ARE MADE IN THE RIGHT PLACE AT THE RIGHT TIME, WHERE THE WAVE OFFERS MAXIMUM STEEPNESS AND POWER.

FOREHAND OFF THE LIP

The forehand off the lip is a fast, radical turn at the top of the wave. Your goal is to use the lip about to break to get back into the wave with maximum speed.
Here are the key steps for a good off the lip:

1. Vertical climb line
Exiting your bottom turn, press hard on your back foot to aim the board towards the lip.

2. Maximum shoulder rotation
Benefit from the projection of your bottom turn to rotate your leading shoulder towards the lip. This rotation helps you flow to the lip and prepare your top turn.

3. Back foot pressure at the lip
Right before the lip, weight your back foot, to allow a rapid direction change on to the rail. Arch your back and look over your leading shoulder to the bottom of the wave.

4. Trigger shoulder counter-rotation
Your upper body rotation launches your off the lip. Begin at the very moment your board starts passing above the lip, with strong back foot pressure. The more dynamic this motion is, the faster your board turns.

5. Push your tail
Push your tail as hard as you can throughout the turn to shift your weight to your front foot. This guarantees a big spray and better flow to your next bottom turn.

Function:
Attack the best zone of the wave, using it to relaunch into the slope.
Goal:
Aim for the lip and through it to accelerate throughout the turn.
Trajectory:
Start the turn with your board flat against the lip. Finish it aiming at the next bottom turn.
Technique:
Keep your upper body straight and strong at the impact with the lip, counter rotate fast, pushing the tail.
Try:
Going into the turn, raise your leading shoulder towards the lip.
Avoid:
Letting your upper body get outside the line at the lip, putting you off balance and leaving you stuck in the lip.

CAUTION: Don't start your counter rotation too early. Instead of an off the lip, you'll have to settle for a weak mid-face turn with less speed.

+ TIP

At the lip, accelerate your movement. This change of rhythm gives momentum to, and emphasizes your turn.

BACKHAND
OFF THE LIP

Compared to your forehand, the transition is more natural at the top of the wave on your backhand. You have the clear advantage of being able to bend your body forwards at the waist. This upside down body motion brings your board into position to take a steep line back down the wave, creating acceleration.

1. Maximum opening of the shoulder axis
Coming out of the bottom turn, target the lip thinking your shoulders are your eyes: They must fully rotate to 'see' your target and take you there. This full shoulder axis rotation will then be useful at the top when completing your turn.

2. Bend forward before closing the shoulder axis
When in the last third of the climb, start bending forwards. To facilitate the upside down motion of your upper body, start looking towards the bottom of the wave.

3. Close the shoulder axis
Once your body is upside down, apply all your power. Throw your front shoulder towards the bottom of the wave, pushing hard on the back foot to give impact to your maneuver. Do not try to recover too early - wait at least until mid-face.

Function:
Attack the best zone of the wave, using it to relaunch into the slope.
Goal:
Bend your body forward and upside down to accelerate.
Trajectory:
Start the turn with your board flat against the wave and vertical. Finish it aiming at the next bottom turn.
Technique:
At the top bend forward, counter rotating and applying back foot pressure.
Try:
Waiting until you are upside down before applying maximum power.
Avoid:
Going into counter rotation before bending forwards.

➕ TIP

For a 'twelve o'clock', vertical off the lip, aim your front arm above the lip when reaching the top third of the wave. Your palm should be turned towards the lip and held higher than your elbow.

1

FINS OUT RE-ENTRY

The fins out is an extreme off the lip which has become an absolute must in a modern surfer's repertoire. Unlike a regular off the top, the goal is to delay the turn and make the board rotate above the lip. Try it in fairly powerful waves when you spot a nice foamy section or a little lip starting to break.

1. Aim above the lip
Extend your bottom turn looking to reach above the lip. As the lip breaks forward it is going to help push you back into the wave.

2. Create 'pop'
As the board passes the lip, press hard on the tail to pop it out of the lip, gaining amplitude and momentum.

3. Forward weight shift
Start your rapid upper body rotation when your fins pass above the lip or the foam - instantly shifting all your weight forward. This dynamic transfer is key to totally releasing pressure on the fins, allowing the pop that releases the tail.

4. Control the release
Focus on the bottom of the wave to aid control and recovery.
Stay low and close to your board.
When you have reached your full extension, apply back foot pressure to engage the fins, giving you back control of your trajectory.

Function:
To project over the lip, exploring the wave's limits.
Goal:
To get your fins and tail rotating out above the lip.
Trajectory:
Vertical, above the lip.
Technique:
Generating pop, rotating and recovering.
Try:
Aiming up above the lip, kick out your tail.
Avoid:
Getting your weight too far back, which will prevent pop and impede control.

✚ TIP

Wait until you have accumulated enough energy through back foot pressure before you release the tail.

CUTBACKS

A CUTBACK IS USEFUL
WHEN YOU ARE GOING
FASTER THAN THE WAVE.
YOU NEED TO GET BACK
TO THE CURL, IN ORDER
TO RECONNECT WITH
THE WAVE'S RHYTHM AND
GAIN THE SPEED YOU NEED
FOR YOUR NEXT TURN.

CUTBACK

The aim of the cutback is to reposition yourself back in the maximum energy zone of the wave, with the goal of drawing your arc across all the available wave height.
This turn is particularly adapted to pushy waves without much wall, where the wave gives you speed but limited options for maneuvers. A strong, functional cutback should reposition you back in the curl, until you spot the next section to use.

Extend your bottom turn to the top of the shoulder to create sufficient space for your full rail cutback.

There are two main parts to a good cutback:

1. Step 1: Intense turn

Once at the top of the shoulder, lean over your heel side rail and hold it underwater evenly spreading pressure on both legs.

Your goal is to intensify this rail pressure to drive through your turn: progressively lower your center of gravity throughout the high part of the turn, touching the water with your leading hand.

2. Step 2: Gain another slope

Remember to tighten your turn upwards towards the foam, so that you keep some slope to complete the last phase of the cutback.

Release the rail putting your board flat just before you reach the foam. Then, transfer to the opposite rail as you connect with the foam, so that it pushes you back out. You can then finish with a down slope, ready to link your next bottom turn.

Function:
Get back to the curl to reconnect with the wave.
Goal:
Draw your arc as big as possible, without any break in the curve.
Trajectory:
Draw a "S" shape line across all the available wave height.
Technique:
Get your board flat and transfer rails before hitting the foam.
Try:
Lower your center of gravity throughout the down turn.
Avoid:
Being stiff and jerky with rail pressure.

+ TIP

Going in fits and starts kills both speed and style.
Focus on smoothly managing the intensity of your rail pressure, drawing a flowing line.

ROUNDHOUSE CUTBACK

The roundhouse cutback is one of the longest lines to draw on a surfboard. Perfectly adapted to weak waves without much wall, it is a return to the curl extended into an off the top rebound. It not only reconnects you to the curl, but also gives you an opportunity to create speed off the rebound. First, you need to create some space - make a wide bottom turn towards the top of the shoulder.

Three steps make a successful roundhouse cutback:

1. Maximize the drop line

Once at the top of the shoulder, immediately bend your legs pushing on your inside rail. To make the most of the drop line, evenly apply your leg pressure along the rail and touch the water.
Where you look is essential. Avoid looking at the white water too early: you'll end up cutting your line short, not extracting maximum speed and amplitude.

2. Drive off the bottom

Once at the bottom, try to find the natural extension of the arc, linking it smoothly into driving off the bottom. Intensify pressure on the rail to tighten your line and drive your board back up.

3. Rebound high

Driving off the bottom, now target the rebound zone you want to hit: Extend your body and open your shoulder axis to facilitate your climb. Aim as high as possible, so that you rebound off the top with maximum steepness and speed.
For a strong rebound, contract your abdominals and push the board flat against the white water. Your goal is to re-enter the wave, instead of being absorbed by it: Be active through the rebound, making sure you push through the turn rather than just turn.
As the foam carries you, rotate your shoulder axis back towards the bottom of the wave. Lower your center of gravity to accelerate out with control.

Function:
Return to the curl gaining maximum speed and amplitude off the top.
Goal:
Make the widest possible unbroken arc, be positive with your rebound to re-enter wave with more speed.
Trajectory:
A 'figure 8' across all the available wave height, punctuated with a strong, radical rebound.
Technique:
Lower your center of gravity throughout the down turn, maintain constant rail pressure through the climb, push the turn through rebound.
Try:
Initially aiming for a spot at the bottom of the wave to accelerate and extend your line around it.
Avoid:
Aiming at the white water behind you too soon. Also avoid multiple pumps through your arcs.

✚ TIP

The cutback is not a power struggle. Rather, a kind of caress on the wave with controlled, progressive pressure.
Start by setting your rail in the wave, then lower your center of gravity to maintain flow.

CARVE

Particularly suited to powerful waves with open sections, the carve is a power turn performed in the pocket. The goal is to put all your power and weight on the rail to dramatically change your line and direction, emphasizing your own speed, control and power.

1. Power against power

When going fast on a powerful wave, you need to stamp your authority on the face to be able to arc your line. You should feel the wave's power and offer sufficient power of your own in return in order to maintain control of your line.

Initial push: Start the maneuver by pushing hard on your heel side rail, without turning your shoulders. Your goal is to bury the rail in the wall to absorb its power. Instead of freeing the power of your shoulder axis rotation too early, push on your legs and look above your shoulder, sticking your leading hand in the wave.

Follow up rotation: Once strong and stable on your rail, accelerate the shoulder axis rotation by pushing hard on your heels. Make sure to give all your back foot power, extending your leg.

2. Transition into bottom turn

Once the carve is executed, release the rail getting your board flat before reaching the foam and aim for the bottom in order to use the remaining slope and prepare for your next bottom turn.

Function:
To cut your line and stay in the curl.
Goal:
Stamp your authority on the wave, 'cutting it in half' with your rail.
Trajectory:
180° curve on the wall.
Technique:
Apply intense and spontaneous rail pressure in an arc, releasing before hitting the white water.
Try:
Entering the turn with your shoulder axis closed, in order to free its power of rotation later in the turn.
Avoid:
Still being on your inside rail when reaching the foam.

+ TIP

For a stronger, flowing arc throughout, focus on making a vertical carve into the next bottom turn, rather than a horizontal carve into the foam.

LAYBACK SNAP

The layback snap is a radical, abrupt turn. Useful for suddenly cutting your trajectory, you can execute it in the pocket or against a section coming at you. A tight radius turn that bleeds speed spectacularly, it varies your repertoire, showing spontaneity and power.

1. All on the back foot

Before pushing hard on your back foot, stick your trailing arm into the wave, lowering your center of gravity and helping get on the rail suddenly. Then apply all your back foot power, pushing the tail into the wave. Get all your power above your fins, making a big spray and getting a strong sensation of controlled aggression.

2. Layback

To be able to free all your power, you must literally sit or layback on the wave. Release the tail and push it out as hard as you can until your back leg is straight. Simultaneously bring your front knee up to your chest to keep your board close and under control.

3. Recover

To recover your trajectory and stance, release back foot pressure still keeping your board close with your front leg flexed. What you cannot yet release are your abdominals- you need them strong to stand back up. Keep your knees bent until the wave starts catching you up, benefit from its push to help you stand back up.

Function:
Dramatically cut your trajectory.
Goal:
Push your tail underwater, releasing it with maximum back leg power making a big spray.
Trajectory:
A 90° degree angle.
Technique:
Lower your center of gravity suddenly, pushing hard over your fins.
Try:
Sticking your back arm in the water before pushing and extending your back leg.
Avoid:
Keeping your front leg straight when pushing.

+ TIP

Lay right back on the wave face, trust it to help you stand back up.

FLOATER

THE FLOATER IS SUITED
TO FAST WAVES THAT DROP
SECTIONS IN FRONT OF YOU.
IT INVOLVES RIDING
OVER THE ROOF OF A SECTION
TO KEEP SPEED AND RHYTHM.
THIS RIDE OVER THE LIP
OR FOAMY SECTION BRINGS
A LIGHT, FLOATING FEELING.

FLOATER

The floater involves gliding horizontally over the lip or foamy section breaking in front of you.
Your goal is to ride over the section in order to reconnect with the open face.

1. Board flat over the lip
As the wave is about to section ahead, don't hesitate: Fully extend your body to get your board flat over the lip.
Try to approach the lip with a 45° angle to optimize gliding towards the shoulder.

2. Glide light
Having placed your board flat above the lip, free your upper body, making yourself light and loose.
Shift your weight forward to glide longer.
Savor this floating sensation, prolonging your glide by turning your shoulder axis towards the outside.

3. Project to the flats
This floating feeling can't last forever. As you lose speed, your tail starts dropping - the signal to apply pressure to the board and project your upper body towards the flats. The more you have turned your shoulders to the outside in the preceding gliding phase, the more momentum you'll have to amplify your projection.
Remember to bend your knees to absorb the landing.

Function:
To glide over a section keeping speed and regaining the curl.
Goal:
Glide over the lip as long as possible, maximizing projection.
Trajectory:
Horizontal, over the curtain or foamy section.
Technique:
Maintain a loose upper body above the lip, turning the shoulders towards the outside. The following counter-rotation amplifies projection.
Try:
As the board slows and tail drops, weight your back foot and project your upper body towards the flats.
Avoid:
Rotating shoulders too early to the flats.

+ TIP

To extend the floater try to quickly pump / release the board.
Project your arms towards the flats when it's time to land.

FOAM CLIMB

The foam climb involves climbing up and over a foamy white water section at a 45° angle. It is useful when you are caught behind a broken crumbly section and need to catch up. Because of the white water you don't have enough room to perform a good bottom turn, and it's time to climb the foam.

Short intense pressure:
Without the time and space to draw a long bottom turn to the top of the wave, you need an immediate climb. Give intense leg pressure to instantly sink your inside rail under water, then release it early to make the board pop up before the foam swallows it.

Total extension:
The extension is the key phase of your foam climb. Your extension needs to be full and exaggerated, to get as light as you possibly can. Amplify the extension by raising both arms and arching your back to the sky. Simultaneously bring your front knee to your chest, dragging your board with you.

Grip the foam:
Once your board starts climbing the foam, put even pressure on it to keep control of the turn. With your legs flexed, stomp the board against the foam as if you wanted to push it back to the outside.

Project the board to the flats:
Maintain strong pressure on your board with your body compact until the foam starts carrying you with it. Then project your upper body down to the flats, keeping your abdominals strong.
Use this projection to keep your board under your feet and land.

Function:
Get past a foamy section that you're caught behind.

Goal:
Stay light to climb fast right to the top of the whitewater.

Trajectory:
45° up the foam.

Technique:
A complete, dynamic extension, control on top of the foam followed by a projection down to the flats.

Try:
Arching your back and raising both arms to aid your climb.

Avoid:
Projecting down from the foam with your upper body without first having pushed your board off the foam.

 TIP

Make sure you've gained full energy and amplitude from the foamy section before projecting back down in recovery.

CLOSEOUT RE-ENTRY

THE CLOSEOUT RE-ENTRY
INVOLVES TURNING OFF
AN ONCOMING SECTION
AS THE WAVE SHUTS DOWN.
AS THE WAVE IS ABOUT
TO CLOSE OUT AHEAD,
YOU COULD BE CONSERVATIVE
AND DECIDE TO KICK OUT
AND PADDLE BACK TO THE LINEUP.
BY PERFORMING THIS MOVE,
YOU INSTEAD DECIDE TO
MAXIMIZE THE AMPLITUDE
AND LENGTH OF YOUR RIDE BY
HITTING THE ONCOMING LIP FOR
MAXIMUM IMPACT.

CLOSEOUT RE-ENTRY

The closeout re-entry is a last-chance maneuver, before the wave totally closes out. It is a radical turn on the section coming at you, a turbulent wave zone that forces you to be aggressive if you want to complete your ride with an exclamation point.

Target the lip
Having taken maximum speed, draw your bottom turn towards the oncoming section. Keep watching the lip and extend your body to flow up in your approach and have maximum power and momentum when hitting the lip.

1. Anticipate lip contact
The lip is coming right at you. The approach you need to take is straightforward: You have to dominate it to avoid getting knocked off.
To avoid being overcome by the lip, anticipate impact by flexing your legs and apply strong back foot pressure just before you hit it.
Your center of gravity must be lower than the board's with your backside under the rail.

2. Contact
It's time to be positive and push your board hard against the wave. Flatten your board against the lip, compressing hard as if you wanted to push it back out.
Simultaneously, the head/shoulder/arm axis must start rotating to take you back into the wave.

3. Projection acceleration
Do not undercook your turn. Your goal is to accelerate with your projection off the lip, to reach the flats and escape before the lip impacts. Keep your legs flexed and strong, and your body compact.
Look at the landing area, so the rest of your body naturally follows the movement.

Landing
The lip should carry you out of the turn. Before reaching the flats, release pressure to get the board underneath your body. Get ready to bend your legs to absorb the turbulent impact of landing. If the wave is really steep, weight your tail to avoid nose-diving.

Try all versions of closeout re-entries:
lay-back: Intensify back foot pressure and layback to make a bigger spray.
reverse: Shift all your weight forward to make a complete reverse using the lip.

Function:
To use the closeout section to re-enter the wave.

Goal:
To hit the lip hard and accelerate out from the impact.

Trajectory:
45° towards the lip, then straight to the wave's base.

Technique:
Anticipate lip impact then give a strong, spontaneous board pressure and rotation against it to project out of the turn.

Try:
Keeping your center of gravity low to emphasize the turn.

Avoid:
Releasing pressure on the lip too early.

+ TIP

Keep a strong, straight back to ease rotation.

1   2   3

360°

SINCE WAVES ARE USUALLY ONLY RIDDEN IN ONE DIRECTION, IT IS BOTH CHALLENGING AND PROGRESSIVE TO COMPLETE FULL ROTATIONS. EITHER BY REVERSING OR CARVING, 360'S ARE RISKY, RADICAL MANEUVERS WHOSE OUTCOME RELIES UPON PERFECT TIMING WITH THE WAVE.

© daniel russo

CARVING 360

As with an off the lip, your goal is to attack and use the lip. In the case of the carving 360, you need to extend and hold your bottom turn on the rail to draw a complete circle on the wave.
Find a wave with enough power and steepness, and connect your board with the feathering lip, which should help you get back into the wave to complete your full circle.

1. Climb beyond vertical
Prepare for a long, strong bottom turn, you should keep pressure on the rail to get beyond vertical before you reach the lip. The lip should then push you to complete your 360° rotation.
Your trailing hand serves like the point of a compass: The more you lean and touch the water, the bigger your circle is.

2. A quick tight turn at the top
As you contact the lip, press hard on your tail, with more weight toe side (or heel side for a backhand carving 360). Simultaneously, accelerate the shoulder axis rotation, this quick movement at the lip helps you get compact and leaning forward into the wave.

3. Secure the drop
Avoid early extension and premature pressure release. To help complete the maneuver, keep crouched and compact with your eyes targeting the bottom until you gain speed down the face.

Function:
Use the critical section of the wave to complete a 360° rotation.
Goal:
Keep inside rail pressure throughout the circle.
Trajectory:
A full circle using the entire wave height.
Technique:
Hold rail pressure from the bottom turn and use maximum shoulder axis rotation to drive the 360.
Try:
Getting to the lip beyond vertical.
Avoid:
Extending at contact with the lip.

 TIP

To help complete the turn, grab the inside rail with your trailing hand when connecting with the lip, keeping you compact. Keep grabbing until your board is back under your body.

REVERSE 360

The reverse is a complete rotation towards the wave's base, involving releasing pressure above the fins to launch the spin.

1. Use the lip
Get to the lip at a 45° angle.
Upon contact, keep pressure on the board conserving momentum, and start rotating your upper body towards the wave's base.

2. Total weight shift
Once going with the lip, you need to free the fins from gripping the wave.
Transfer all your weight to the front and keep rotating your upper body to make the board follow.

3. Lead the reverse
As all your weight goes forward, you get a drifting feeling without the control of your fins. Bend your front leg and touch the water with your leading hand to reverse around it.

4. Maintain control
Start transferring your weight back to the tail before the full rotation is complete, as your fins grip the wave you regain control and drive to be able to go into your next turn.
Stay low and look at the wave base until you feel stable.

Reverses are easier on oncoming sections that help you rotate and spin. Practice on closeout sections before you try reversing on an open face.

Function:
Spin down the wave.
Goal:
Free all pressure on the back foot to release the fins and make the board reverse.
Trajectory:
Reversing throughout the wave's height.
Technique:
Shift weight forwards liberating the fins, rotate around front foot, looking above your leading shoulder to spin.
Try:
Touching the water with your leading hand to initiate the spin.
Avoid:
Keeping your weight too far back at the beginning of the turn, preventing fin release.

 TIP

Grab your rail with your trailing hand to aid control through the spin while looking above your leading shoulder.

INVERTED REVERSE

The inverted reverse is an explosive rotation projected off the lip. The idea is to overpower the projection of the lip, throwing the fins forwards and then completing the spin.

1. Find the target
Your goal is to get projected down to the wave's base.
Connect with a lip with sufficient power and projection.

2. Anticipate contact
Just before reaching the lip, start bending your legs whilst letting the board climb, in order to lower your center of gravity.
Be ready to exert an explosive effort off the lip, getting maximum energy from its projection.

3. Exaggerate the movement
As the lip carries you, project all your weight towards the wave base.
This motion must be pronounced and dynamic, similar to a cartwheel.
Simultaneously, stick your front arm deep in the wall to reverse around it.
Unlike a regular reverse, you need to be upside down under your board with your eyes fixed on the bottom.

4. Pull the rail
The lip will amplify your head down spinning motion.
Pull the outside rail with your trailing hand to accelerate the spin and throw the fins forward.

5. Stick to the board
To recover, stay compact and keep grabbing rail.
The more explosive your projection is, the more momentum you create to finish the reverse.

Function:
Project a vertical reverse rotation.
Goal:
Use the lip for an explosive fin release down the wave.
Trajectory:
Vertical 360° rotation following the lip's projection.
Technique:
Grab and pull the rail with your trailing hand to accelerate the board motion and give it the right trajectory.
Try:
Planting your leading hand as deep as possible in the face.
Avoid:
Getting your weight above the board at contact with the lip.

✚ TIP

Arrive at the lip with board at '12 o'clock', then invert by throwing your fins towards the sky.

AERIALS

ONCE YOU ARE CONSISTENTLY
PERFORMING THE BASIC
FUNDAMENTAL MANEUVERS,
YOU CAN EXPAND YOUR
SURFING HORIZONS TO THE
SPACE ABOVE THE LIP.
DON'T RESTRICT YOURSELF BY
BEING CONSERVATIVE,
AERIAL MANEUVERS ARE THE
NATURAL NEXT STEP IN YOUR
SURFING PROGRESSION.

AERIAL

Pioneered in the early 80's with the advent of light shortboards, the aerial allows you to fly above the wave. This basic flight must be your first goal before you go for all the complicated variations of the aerial repertoire.

1. Preparation

Create maximum speed on a wave with enough wall and power.
Find the section that you will use as a launch pad and aim your bottom turn at it.

2. Launch pad

Keep targeting the section you want to use as a launch pad, and extend your bottom turn to aim above it, with maximum speed. The best launching angle of approach is 45° to the lip.

3. Pop

The height of your air depends on the amount of pop you generate.
Timing is essential: Wait until your nose passes the lip, then give a strong kick on your tail. Follow this tail kick with a quick extension of your body as your fins pass over the lip, launching your air.

4. Fly high

As you launch, completely release the tail pressure, extending your upper body and raising your arms (as if jumping).
Simultaneously, raise your front knee to your chest to bring the board with you. Let yourself climb without commencing your shoulder axis rotation too early. At the same time, avoid letting your upper body lag behind the rest of the movement, by tensing your abdominals or by grabbing the rail.

5. Control the direction

Once at the top of your flight, look towards your landing zone to make your board and body turn as one. Target the whitewater ready to absorb you, rather than the flats.
It's time to get the board back under your body. Aim to have the tail higher than the nose on landing, in order to fit the slope of wave.

6. Smooth landing

Extend your front leg to try and stomp the board on the wave.
As you contact the lip or whitewater, bend your legs to absorb the impact of landing.

Function:
Fly above the wave, passing over a section in the air.
Goal:
Project past the lip, flying over the wave for maximum amplitude of trajectory.
Trajectory:
Launch off the bottom with a 45° angle to the lip.
Technique:
Arch your back and bring front knee to your chest to convert pop into height.
Try:
Keeping your abdominals contracted throughout the aerial.
Avoid:
Extending your legs when launching.

IMPORTANT

There are a wide range of grabs to explore, inspired by skateboarding (mute, lien, stalefish, etc). Beyond their style aspect, they keep you connected to the board during the aerial. Remember to let go of the rail before landing to absorb the shock.

➕ TIP

As with an ollie in skateboarding, give a strong pop on the tail, then release back foot pressure to transfer weight forward. Work on your ollies on a skateboard, to get a better feel of the basics of the movement, then adapt it to the waves.

AIR REVERSE

With the rapid evolution of modern surfing, the air reverse has become an absolute must. It usually involves a 270° air rotation, followed by a backwards landing and a finishing spin as the fins catch the white water.
Once you master the basic aerial, add a rotation to it.

1. Use the lip
Find maximum speed to aid flight.
As you spot your launch pad, aim for it with a 45° bottom turn.

2. Launching
Try reaching the lip with maximum momentum to fly and spin.
Generate a strong pop and engage your shoulder axis rotation.

3. Rotation
An upper body rotation is essential for performing your air reverse.
The stronger the rotation is, the more the board will follow it.
As you launch the air, bring your front knee to your chest. You can also grab the outside rail with your trailing hand. This helps keep you close to your board, and accelerates the rotation.

4. Landing
Focus on landing smoothly, quickly stabilizing the board.
The landing is often backwards, or 'fakie'. Be ready to bend your legs to absorb the impact, as your fins catch the foam they want to make the board spin.
To complete the rotation, stay low and look towards the shore above your front shoulder.
For a textbook air reverse, note that today's very best surfers will opt to let go of the rail before landing, just as skateboarders do. But in the learning stage you can also keep hold of the rail, releasing and standing up once the spin is complete.

CAUTION: A raised front arm hinders rotation, whereas aimed low it serves as a rotation point that the body turns around.

Function:
Execute a forward aerial rotation.
Goal:
Spin in the air above the wave.
Trajectory:
A 270° to 360° rotation in the air, completed upon landing.
Technique:
Engage a strong upper body rotation from the launch, looking for a vertical rotation, rather than horizontal.
Try:
Bringing your front knee to your chest right after launching.
Avoid:
Raising your leading arm.

✚ TIP

When launching, grab the rail to stay compact with your board and aid the rotation.

ALLEY OOP

Developed by Californian Tim Curran in the 90's, the alley-oop is a backwards aerial rotation. Find a wave with enough power and lip projection: The goal is to launch towards the shoulder to complete the backwards rotation in time to re-enter the wave.

1. Use the lip
Timing at the lip is essential - you should use it as a launch pad just as it projects forward, in order to fly in the right direction.

2. Fly towards the shoulder
Push off the lip to create pop right before launching.
At this stage your main focus is to start flying with the right trajectory and not end up behind the wave. After the pop, let the tail lift towards the shoulder and the beach. This initiates the rotation.
At the same time, raise both your front arm and front knee to fly, climb and bring the board with you.

3. Upper body rotation
Once in the air, rotate your head to spot your launching track.
Let your shoulders and arms follow your eyes to accelerate the rotation.
With good core strength both your lower body and board will follow the motion initiated by your upper body.

4. Landing forward
The goal is to complete your rotation in the air to land light and facing forward, with your body over the board.
It will not happen on your first attempt. Begin by landing fakie, finishing your rotations with spins out of the white water.

5. Quickly stabilize
A low center of gravity means stability.
Be ready to absorb the impact of landing by bending your knees.

Function:
Fly backwards in the air.
Goal:
Execute a complete rotation in the air.
Trajectory:
Launch towards the shoulder, followed by a 180° to 360° backwards aerial rotation.
Technique:
Pop the tail towards the beach and shoulder of the wave upon launching, lead the rotation with your head, spotting the landing over your back shoulder early.
Try:
Simultaneously lifting front arm and front knee at the launch.
Avoid:
Trying to gain pure height without also projecting towards the shoulder with your down the line momentum.

Onshore or cross-shore winds help keep the board under your feet as you rotate.

 TIP

In the air, kick your back foot toe side rail to accelerate the board rotation.

4

5

TUBERIDING

TUBERIDING IS THE BEST
EXPERIENCE IN SURFING.
IT INVOLVES RIDING
UNDERNEATH AND THROUGH
A SECTION OF A WAVE THAT
TOTALLY COVERS YOU.
IT IS AN INTENSE MOMENT OF
GRACE AND BEAUTY, WHERE
YOUR RIDE BLENDS IN PERFECT
HARMONY WITH THE WAVE.
YOU FLOW INTO THE WAVE'S
MOST INTIMATE ZONE AT THE
VERY CENTER OF ITS ENERGY,
IN A FLUID, INSTINCTIVE STATE.

FOREHAND TUBE

Tuberiding is a risky maneuver, with minimal margin for error. It consists of riding the deepest part of the curl, totally covered by the throwing lip.

In this critical situation, the surfer must simultaneously combine flow, instinct and control, whilst keeping pinpoint accuracy in his trajectory to blend it into the wave's shape and rhythm.

Tubular waves often involve difficult late take-offs. The best approach is to not waste any tube time by directly getting covered from take-off. The second option is to get to the bottom, and then pull in.

1. Feel the wave

To get tubed, you need to sync your speed with that of the wave. You must look at the lip and evaluate if the wave is going to accelerate or slow down, the key to good tuberiding. You need to gauge how the tube is going to break in fractions of a second in order to adapt your trajectory.

If it accelerates, get busy with short pumps, avoiding getting too high up the face or too low.

If it slows, break your line pointing your board towards the base of the wave. Then as the wave catches you up, adjust your line back to aiming for the shoulder, and get covered.

2. Positioning

The tuberide is not a turn. Move your feet slightly forward to spread your weight evenly and use the fastest part of the rocker.

The confined space inside the tube requires you to make yourself compact. Bend your knees rather than at the waist, and put your trailing hand in the face to get closer and gain control.

3. Vision

The tube exit looks like an eye. Spot and target it constantly throughout the tuberide, aiming at it with both shoulders to keep speed and control over your trajectory.

Adjust your line:

Waves hardly ever break perfectly. Most of the time, fast changes in shape and pace force you to stay alert. You need to feel what is happening and react spontaneously. Keep touching the wave face to properly position yourself.

If you start going up the face, aim the board down to the bottom. If you are getting too low, pump briefly on your inside rail to go up. Avoid ever getting higher than mid-face.

Keep relaxed and supple to absorb all of these changes inside in the tube.

Adjust your speed:

When the wave accelerates, gain speed by pumping just below mid-face to accelerate and eventually come out.

When it slows, stick your arm in the face to control your speed and enjoy more tube time.

Function:

Ride a wave from the inside.

Goal:

Be inside the tube for the maximum possible amount of time.

Trajectory:

Sideways, just under mid-face.

Technique:

Make short rapid pumps to adjust your line and accelerate, drag your trailing hand in the face to slow down.

Try:

Target the exit with both shoulders and eyes.

Avoid:

Closing your eyes and bending at the waist instead of at the knees.

✚ TIP

Focus on stability and speed. Move your feet forward, spreading your stance over the flattest, fastest part of the rocker.

If the wave is going to close out and you have time, try to exit by the 'doggy door,' strongly weighting your back foot to break your line and point your board to shore.

BACKHAND
TUBE

As you turn your back to the wave, the need for speed and vision inside the tube forces you to re-orientate your body. The grab rail or 'pig dog' remains to this day the most reliable and commonly used technique. It consists in turning both shoulders towards the exit while grabbing the outside rail with the trailing hand. Body weight should be evenly spread over both feet, and upper body straightened up to ensure stability and vision.

When taking off on hollow waves like Teahupoo or Pipeline, it is a clear advantage to be on the heel side rail and grab the rail immediately, to pull the board in a horizontal trajectory under the lip. Things get more complicated when you miss the direct entry and go into a bottom turn. It is then much harder to adjust your speed and trajectory to get under the lip.

The ideal situation is to read the wave well before take-off to position yourself behind the peak and pull straight into the tube.

Gain maximum time:
During take-off, you want to get down the face immediately and out of the projecting lip. Always give an extra paddle, with chest and chin down on the board to tip it down the wave face. Then stay compact, keeping your hands close to the rails and your eyes on the bottom.

Stick to the face:
Once dropping down the wave, turn sideways before reaching mid face to get compact and get covered by the lip.
To accelerate this process, pull on your outside rail with trailing hand. Stick your leading hand in the wave to tighten the turn.

Positioning:
As you get covered, straighten your back and stick your chest out, trying to spread your weight evenly along the board. Your legs should be bent with your back knee tucked in.
Feel all the wave's power and acceleration, the rush is priceless.

Constantly target the exit:
Both shoulders and your eyes should be aiming at the exit at all times. Stay alert to keep control of your line inside the tube, just under mid-face.

Adjust your trajectory:
To go up the face and get closer to the wave, lift your front shoulder towards the wave while simultaneously pulling on your outside rail.
To go down, lower your front shoulder whilst pushing on your front foot.

Type of board
For deeper, controlled tuberides, pick a sleek thruster. A narrow pintail holds well in the face and secures your trajectory even in extreme situations.

Function:
Ride a wave from the inside.
Goal:
Be inside the tube for the maximum possible amount of time.
Trajectory:
Sideways, just under mid-face.
Technique:
Roll your back knee in, chest out, grabbing your outside rail with your trailing hand.
Try:
Aim at the exit with both shoulders, keeping your front shoulder higher.
Avoid:
Closing your eyes and bending at the waist instead of at the knee.

VARIATION: The no grab backhand barrel is the supreme maneuver in surfing. Mastered by the late 3-time world champion Andy Irons, it is the ultimate way to ride the tube. Even after years of tuberiding, only very few can afford the luxury of letting go of the rail.

+ TIP

If there is no exit, try to get as far away from your board as possible by pushing it away. Try to penetrate low enough in the wall to get a chance of popping out behind the wave, rather than going over the falls.

6.
BECOME A COMPLETE SURFER

For the surf addict, surfing is much more than a sport, and means more than just doing good turns.

t is a lifestyle that shapes his or her very existence. The idea is to live by your passion for surfing, embracing every new experience. Each one brings a promise of self-fulfillment.

A UNIQUE PATH

The greatest asset of a surfer is the natural world. Surfing is pursued in a natural environment, non-linear and unrestricted, with the only rules being to respect the ocean and the other surfers. Our blue planet, two thirds covered by ocean, offers each surfer an almost infinite playground with a wealth of experiences.

THE QUEST FOR THE PERFECT WAVE

From the very first wave, the surfer gets addicted to the pure sensation of riding this natural energy. He feels he must always seek to renew it, by taking another wave, and then another better one, and so on. That is the essence of surfing; to find the best wave, to ride as best you can and make the most of its energy to get maximum pleasure.

This quest for the perfect wave changes the surfer's life. It takes him beyond his home spot, from one discovery to the next, even to the most renowned and legendary waves on the planet.

Each surfer follows his own path towards new waves and sensations. The goal is to learn, progress, and live out a maximum of experiences to stay connected to the pure feeling of riding a wave and being at one with the ocean. This process also happens to be fulfilling for him as a person. Beyond a merely sporting progression, he learns more about himself and his surroundings. He encounters nature, people and their different cultures, developing an appreciation and understanding of them.

FOLLOW YOUR OWN PATH

Each surfer defines his own path, according to his situation and preferences, and chooses how he advances into new experiences.

The most important thing is to live surfing to the fullest.

Travel to new spots: Each new wave is an untapped source of pleasure and discoveries.

Become versatile: Spend as much time as possible in the water, to develop your skills and to be at ease in all conditions. Rights, lefts, big, small, hollow, mushy, etc.

Challenge premium waves: Look to surf the best spots on the best days. You could catch the wave of your life. Whether going to the next spot up the coast or a world class destination (Hawaii, Indonesia, Australia, etc), set yourself challenges beforehand and get stuck in when you are there.

Expand your repertoire of maneuvers: Try all turns in all types of waves. Start with the wave entry, then work on them one by one, always going faster, higher, lower, further and deeper.

Become creative: Draw your own lines, imagining infinite combinations of turns. Discover your favorite maneuver.

Look for the magic stick: Curiosity will not kill the cat. Stay open minded and embrace diversity in order to settle on a good quiver of boards that will suit your style and your needs.

Share your sessions: Nothing beats the experience of a good session shared with friends, and the animated exchanging of stories that follows.

Dream about surfing: The best ideas might be born out of the water, before then being fulfilled in the waves.

EXPRESS YOUR STYLE

Your style is your own personal expression of your relationship with the wave and your surfing lifestyle.
It is the imprint you leave on the wave, making you unique and individual.
Your style develops naturally as time and experiences go by.

BE INSPIRED, BE YOURSELF

You cannot learn nor copy style. It is a combination of your personality and the decisions you make on a wave. Yet, in order to develop, it must also feed off outside influences: The best surfers, videos, the spots your surf, the surfboards you ride. Immerse yourself in your own surfing experiences whilst also staying open to all the style influences around you. Your personality will filter and assimilate what suits you best.
Look to the best surfers as the best sources of inspiration to develop your style. Observe and inspire from their vision of surfing and how they use a wave, particularly the subtleties and details. Then adopt the best bits in your own way without copying or losing your natural spontaneity.

EXPLORE DIFFERENT APPROACHES

As time and technical progression go by, you will naturally choose an approach that governs your style.
Aggressive approach: The will to challenge and dominate waves develops a powerful radical style, often in the wave's most critical parts, resulting in a committed, physical surfing style.
Smooth approach: The search for harmony and symbiosis with the wave develops a smooth, fluid style, often in the blue parts of the wave, resulting in a more flowing surfing style.
In reality, a surfer discovers his own compromise between the two approaches, finding his own happy medium.
Explore both and define yours.

THE SURFBOARD: THE TOOL OF STYLE

The choice of surfboard has a big influence upon style. A small, thin board encourages a radical aggressive style, whilst bigger and thicker boards (longboards, minimals, fish, etc) encourage a smoother, flowing style.

ADAPT YOUR TECHNIQUE TO THE WAVE

Style is futile when out of context with the wave. A surfer out of sync with the wave is like a dancer out of rhythm with music. He looks ugly, constantly making jerky movements and adjustments to keep balance, rather than expressing any style.

ATTACK NEW ZONES, TRY NEW MOVES

When pushing your limits, you disrupt your usual, habitual movements and demand a reorganization of your body language.
Your goal is to do hard things, giving the impression that they are easy.

✚ TIP

Love and develop your style, embrace the fact that it is unique to you.
Video is your best friend and your harshest critic. Regularly get filmed to evaluate your style and spot the movements you want to change on the wave. This appraisal makes you identify and address important details.

Your body is your vehicle for physical expression in the surf, and also sets your limits. Dedicate it to the wave and get fit.

WARMING UP

Warming up is necessary to be 100% ready from your first wave. The goal is to raise your heart rate and stimulate the muscles and joints needed in the surf.
They need to be ready to transmit your full power, react to your decisions and protect you from the risk of injury.

How?
On the beach start with 5-10 minutes light jogging. Then go into sit-ups, then stretch your body by replicating the main surfing movements to their full extent: Arm wheels for paddling, upper body rotations, leg squats and push ups.
Carefully warm up your main joints: Ankles, knees, hips, shoulders and neck.

STRETCHING

Stretching serves to loosen muscle and accelerates the recovery process after a physical effort.
On the wave, flexibility is a precious quality.
It eases movements, and helps expressing your style at maximum amplitude, power and speed. The more flexible you are, the quicker your muscles react in urgent situations, to ensure better control and balance.
Stretching should be done daily, throughout life. It encourages flexibility, prevents injury and contributes to everyday well-being.

How?
Before surfing (see Warming Up), or at night after a warm shower or bath, try to stretch the muscles you have worked out, preferably seated or lying down, from head to toe.
For each muscle, first take a deep breath in then stretch progressively whilst breathing out slowly. Release slightly to take in another breath, then start stretching and exhaling. Repeat at least three long breathing cycles for each muscle. Listen to your body. Feel each muscle stretch, and focus on the muscles that need it most.
Note that closing your eyes will help you focus inwardly, and concentrate better on each muscle.

PHYSICAL ATTRIBUTES TO DEVELOP OUT OF THE WATER

ATTRIBUTE	APPLICATION IN THE SURF	EXERCISES
SPEED: Giving rapid explosive muscle reactions in a short time period.	Taking-off, to jump to your feet quickly. On the wave, to generate speed and quickly link radical maneuvers.	Jumping squat thrusts. Abdominal crunches. Sprints, jumping, push-ups, boxing, racket sports (e.g. tennis, squash).
STRENGTH: Muscular power, force and resistance.	For power surfing, putting and holding the board on a rail, driving through turns and meeting the wave's power to execute and complete maneuvers.	Circuit training engaging the whole body. Abdominal core strengthening. Weight training (not before 17 years old).
STAMINA: Ability to endure long lasting efforts.	For postponing fatigue and extending your sessions, allowing you to surf more waves, thus accelerating your progress.	Steady or split effort lasting more than 20 minutes (swimming, jogging, biking).
SUPPLENESS: Executing a full range of movements with control and agility.	For optimum control, balance, choice of trajectories and maneuvers performed with coordination, gracefulness and efficiency of movement.	Proprioception and balance exercises. Stretching, yoga, ballet.

Caution: Do not rush into doing new exercises. First consult an expert who will explain key techniques for each exercise, proposing a personal program suited to you and your body.

ALTERNATIVES

For surfers who don't enjoy gyms or 'exercise for the point of exercise', favorite activities include: skateboarding, bodysurfing, swimming, yoga and martial arts.

NOTE: All these exercises will optimize your overall physical performance, but always keep the big picture in mind: That the best techniques, skills and fitness for surfing are developed by spending time out in the surf.

➕ TIP

There are thousands of ways to help your surfing and improve your physical ability. The key is to seek exercises that mirror surfing, always staying as close as possible to the movements and physical attributes required in the surf.

COMPETITION

A bove all, competition should be fun. It is a good way to progress and boost your adaptability.

PRACTICALITIES

A heat usually lasts 20 minutes and involves 2 to 4 surfers, with half the field making it to the next round, until the final.

Each surfer's performance is tallied on the total score of his two best waves, waves being scored between 0 and 10 points. The surfer with the best total wins the heat and advances.

Judges expect a succession of varied risky and radical maneuvers performed with speed, power and flow.

PREPARATION

Know the spot prior to the event: Surf and study the break at all tides and under all conditions to know the wave and know how it can change.

Get used to competitive constraints: Surf training heats with time limits and specific scoring goals. Take risks and work on maneuvers that could make the difference on the day.

Know your quiver: Try your boards at the contest spot. Pick your most reliable one, the most versatile and suited to the spot.

ADAPTATION

At a contest you have no control over the location, the timing of your heats, other competitors or the conditions on the day.

To stay in the game, you must be ready to adapt and give your best, or even surpass yourself.

Do not start recalling how good the waves were last week. Adapt now.

ROUTINE

Arrive at least an hour and a half prior to your heat with at least two boards, and focus on what you have to do.

Focus on the spot one hour before the heat: Observe how the break changes, the tide, the swell, the heats. Where are the best waves?

Do you need to anticipate surfing your heat on a different peak?

Watch the previous heats: Which positioning and type of surfing is being most rewarded by the judges? Visualize yourself on the best scoring rides.

Warm-up surf: Try the spot out without overdoing it. Feel out the conditions, your board and yourself. Spot the best waves. Leave the water after a good wave with a good feeling.

Strategy: Fifteen minutes before the heat, decide where to position yourself, which waves you want to catch, and how you want to surf them (give yourself a goal). Identify a Plan B in case conditions change. Pick up your jersey and benefit from your paddling out time to take in useful last-minute information.

DURING THE HEAT

Patience: Stay focused on your wave selection. Have the patience to wait for the waves that can make the difference, if possible better than the ones your opponents pick.

Risk taking: Try risky maneuvers that you have successfully been practicing during training.

Blow up: Show your best skills and winning attitude. It's by willing yourself to go fast and dominate that you use all the wave's potential, aiming at its critical sections and linking your maneuvers with precision.

RESULT

Whatever the outcome, be sporting and accept the judges' decision. Each loss has its explanation. Without blaming the judges, your board or bad luck, ask yourself what was missing in your strategy or technique. Go back and practice to progress and make the difference next time. Even if you win, ask yourself questions because your next heat may well be harder.

The competitive path
Club competition → State → Regional → National → Continental → International (ISA, ASP).

PRESSURE

Stress can accompany surfing heats, but don't let it overwhelm you. No matter how calm they appear, your opponents will be feeling it too. Pressure increases when you focus on things you cannot control: the scores, your opponents' surfing, the conditions.

Channel it by focusing on what you need to do and what you can control: Your routine, your strategy, your wave selection, your own surfing.

✛ TIP

Look for and find the bombs, they make the job easier.

CHALLENGE AND COMMITMENT

Every spot has its headline swells and its legendary sessions. And at times, every surfer must confront their fears in big waves.
This moment of truth is anchored in surf culture as a prerequisite to becoming a complete surfer.
Of course, the notion of big waves is relative, and varies from one surfer to another.
Every surfer explores his own limits and sets their own threshold between pleasure and fear. Some never get near it, others push it to the extreme.
Despite this, one absolute certainty remains: The energy of a big wave or tube leaves no one indifferent. They provide intense sensations that can only be felt by confronting them.

FEAR MUST EXIST

Big wave riding is no joke. When the elements rage, the ocean becomes hostile and dangerous.
The best approach is to let pleasure and fear mix and balance each other out.
On one side, the will to take a big wave and have fun pushes you to commit.
But on the other hand, fear and survival instincts force you to stay humble and be conservative.
Awareness of danger makes you take calculated risks without neglecting any detail.
You must use your fear to surf smart and not make reckless decisions.

TRUSTWORTHY GEAR

More than in any other conditions, your surfboard must be reliable.
Use a board suited to the waves that you know and trust.
Opt for a longer, thicker board that paddles faster and offers earlier, easier take-offs, with thin and narrow extremities to give control and hold on the wave.
Use a good leash suited to the power of the spot. Ideally, its length should equal the size of the waves.

BENCHMARK WAVES

Waves renowned for testing and proving surfer's commitment.

1 **Waimea Bay,** 2 **Pipeline,** 3 **Sunset Beach,** 4 **Mavericks,** 5 **Todos Santos,** 6 **Puerto Escondido,** 7 **Teahupoo,** 8 **la Gravière,**
9 **Menakos,** 10 **Nazaré,** 11 **Supertubos,** 12 **Jardim do Mar,** 13 **el Quemao,** 14 **Dungeons,** 15 **The Box...**

CHALLENGE AND COMMITMENT

GOLDEN RULE:

TAKE YOUR TIME ON THE BEACH

Having assessed the swell size, take at least three minutes of observation per foot of wave.
Locate where the big sets break: Big waves do not all break the same way in the same zone.
Feel the trend in the swell: Carefully observe the surf zone, and take time to verify if there are clean up sets which break further out and take surfers by surprise.
Identify your waves: Know which ones you want and the ones you absolutely do not want. Only decide to paddle out once you have identified waves to surf and have fun on.
Observe other surfers in the water: Are you of a similar level?

Choose where to sit
Establish your exit plan
Double check your leash

IN THE WAVES

When first arriving in the lineup position yourself on the shoulder to watch a few waves and rides from the side.
Start by taking some in between waves at the shoulder to slowly build your confidence.
Once you feel good on your board, get progressively closer to the peak.
At the peak watch the horizon carefully to spot any bigger sets and anticipate paddling out or towards the channel, if needed.

CHOOSE THE RIGHT WAVE

Opt for quality over quantity: Bad wave selection can put you in a bad situation. Furthermore, five decent waves on a solid day will often make your session, and exhaust you more than fifty on an average day.

DO NOT QUESTION YOURSELF

DURING TAKE-OFF

It's too late to hesitate, stay focused, commit.
Give maximum paddling effort, sticking your chest and chin to your board.
Take-off early ahead of the wave.
Take the right line keeping balanced and centered on your board, body compact.

CAUGHT INSIDE

At a certain size and power, duck-diving gets impossible. The wave turbulence is too powerful, and your bigger board is impossible to sink underwater. The required technique is to bail under the wave without the board.
Before diving protect your board
Landing lip: Turn your board fins up, placing it parallel to the wave, to reduce the chances of the lip guillotining it in half.
Rolling whitewater: Turn it perpendicular to the foam, to reduce the dragging forces of the turbulence.

FEAR IS OK, BUT DON'T PANIC

The actual time spent underwater during a wipeout is often less than 7 seconds and almost never exceeds 15 seconds. While a 30 second dive is a piece of cake in a pool, you must resist the urge to panic after a few seconds under a wave. The main danger is to fight against the wave's energy, trying to surface too early and quickly using up your oxygen reserves.
Instead, keep calm and go passive underwater. Since the turbulence is powerful, better to go with it and let it take you away from the next wave's impact. Without resisting or trying to surface too early, let 3 to 4 seconds go by, staying totally relaxed. You then preserve maximum oxygen to calmly swim to the surface once the turbulence loses its intensity.
Confronted by a multiple wave set, you will have to repeat the above. Let each wave of the set take you further and further from the impact zone. Recover, breathe deeply, and get back to the lineup avoiding lingering in the impact zone.

✚ TIP

Trust your intuition as a guide in big waves and proceed step-by-step. When fear takes over and pleasure disappears, don't force yourself.

7.
TO KNOW AND RESPECT

Surfing is an individual sport that brings a profound, at times selfish pleasure.

Yet, the surfing act demands you to be mindful of others and your environment, as much as of yourself. Each individual surfer belongs to a broader community, which he must respect to fit in and find his balance.

As with any sport, surfing entails certain risks. These can be reduced, with prevention always the best cure.

SYMPTOM	PREVENTION/TREATMENT
Surfer's Ear Over time, internal ear cartilage grows in response to the pressure difference caused by cold and wind. This reduces the auditory canal and holds water inside causing earaches and reducing hearing.	Use earplugs. Contact a specialist.
Lower back pain (Lumbago) Caused by an arched paddling position that stresses the lower back muscles.	Stretching. Regular core abdominal exercises to balance the skeleton, strengthen, restore posture and prevent pain.
Ankle and knee sprains and fractures Caused by awkward landing of maneuvers, e.g. on the flats, or the impact of the lip.	Warm up. Wax your board carefully. Learn to land (be ready to bend legs to absorb the shock of landing). Avoid landing at all costs in very critical situations. Strengthen leg muscles.
Shoulder dislocation In event of a bad wipeout and/or shoulder weakness.	Specific shoulder muscle strengthening.
Rashes Caused by friction with wetsuit, surfboard or boardshorts.	Apply cream or Vaseline to rash-exposed zones.
Cuts, fractures Caused by surfboard.	Learn to fall far from your surfboard, preferably tucked up protecting head with arms. Use a rubber nose tip (Nose Guard).
Cuts, traumas, fractures Caused by the sea bed, rocks, reef.	In shallow waters, fall horizontally while protecting head. On coral or rock bottom, do not make jerky kicking movements towards the bottom to surface. Use reef boots.
Sunburn	Bring an umbrella, hat or cap to the beach. Apply waterproof high protection sunscreen (over 30spf at least), on face, arms and back. Wear a wetsuit or UV protecting rash vest.
Hypothermia Caused by body thermal shock when water and air temperatures differ greatly.	Gradually enter the water: first wet arms and neck to get your body used to temperature difference.
Dehydration, fatigue	Drink water before each session. During long sessions, take 10 to 15 minutes breaks every two hours to recharge your batteries.

NOTE:
A healthy diet and lifestyle along with regular physical training contribute to lower risks of injury linked to fatigue.

THE SURF TRAVEL MEDICAL KIT

Before you go, make sure you have all required vaccines. In particular, some countries require the yellow fever vaccine.
Arm yourself with a complete medical kit and consult your doctor who will customize it to your destination:
Cuts, infections: Antiseptic products, antibiotic ointments, gauze bandages, band-aids, sterile gauze swabs, adhesive tape, scissors.
Sea urchins: Needle, tweezers, little mirror.
Sprains: Adhesive tape (non elastic), Tiger Balm.
Rashes: Vaseline.
Sunburn: Waterproof, high protection sunscreen (30 spf minimum), after sun cream, moisturizer.
Mosquito bites: Mosquito repellent, net, coils.
Earaches: Consult your doctor.
Digestion problems: Consult your doctor.
Allergies: Consult your doctor.
Pain, fever, headaches: Paracetamol, thermometer.
Sexually transmitted diseases: Condoms.

 TIP

Depending on where you are abroad, avoid drinking tap water in favor of bottled or filtered water.

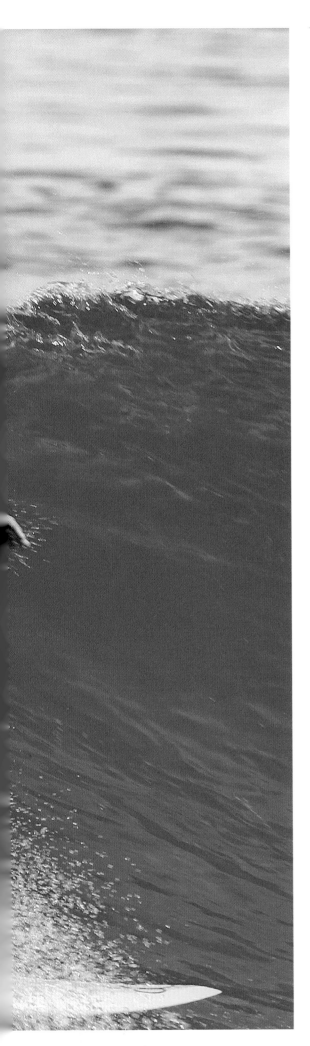

SAFETY
AND ETIQUETTE

RESPECTING PRIORITY RULES

There should only be one surfer per wave.
The first rule of respect is never to drop in on a surfer already riding the wave, or take-off behind him.
Wave breaking one way, left or right:
The surfer taking-off the closest to the initial breaking point of the wave has priority.
Wave breaking both ways, a peak:
Two surfers can split the peak, if they take opposite directions without getting in each other's way. The first surfer up has priority. A second surfer can go the opposite way on the same wave.
Two separate waves meet up:
When two separate waves meet up, the surfer arriving first should kick out first to avoid collision.

SAFETY

Before surfing:
- Assess the conditions, locate dangers, make entry and exit plans.
- If in any doubt, ask someone on the beach or in the water.
- Avoid surfing by yourself, unless someone is watching from the beach.
- At a beach with lifeguards, check flag colors and meanings. Always avoid surfing inside a swimming area.
In the waves:
- Avoid being in anyone's way, especially the deepest surfer on the peak. Do not paddle in anyone's way, or keep paddling for the wave once someone has taken it.
- As you paddle out, avoid being in the trajectory of a surfer riding a wave. Paddle around the surf zone to avoid being in anyone's way.
- The surfer on a wave must do his best to avoid a surfer paddling out. Avoid going for a risky maneuver right above him or trying to spray him. Go around or kick out.
- The surfer paddling out must do his best to keep hold of his board and avoid letting it go towards a surfer on the wave or any surfer paddling behind him.

SHARING

In the waves
- Do not try to catch every wave.
- Do not immediately reposition yourself deepest at the peak after having taken a wave while the other surfers wait for their turn.
- Give a wave to someone every once in a while.
- Encourage and look after the youngest surfers.

UNWRITTEN RULES

Each surf spot carries its own surf culture, and its own codes. Some locations might be welcoming with an infinity of waves to catch. But the rules change at popular and busy spots.
Having to deal with the overcrowding of their spot, some local surfers consider that they have priority over visitors, and a certain pecking order naturally takes place. If you are visiting a spot, respect the locals, and approach the spot calmly. Avoid positioning yourself straight at the peak, and wait for your turn. This unwritten rule prevails at most surf destinations on the planet, and you have to accept it when traveling. However, even at the most crowded spots, with respect for the locals, patience and humility, it is always possible to get your wave, and enjoy your moment.
On your next surf trip, remember to adopt a calm approach in the line-up, with respect for the pecking order, patience and a good positive vibe, in order to fit in.

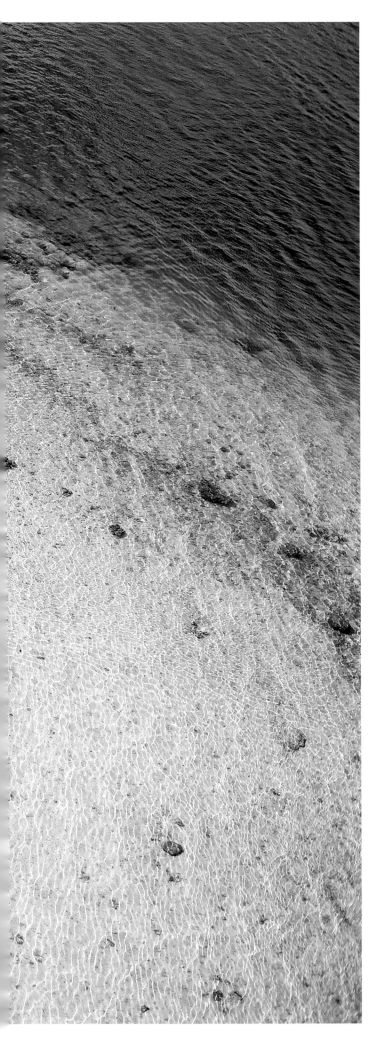

ENVIRONMENT

"If we love our waves, beaches and oceans, the least we can do is pass them on to our children as beautiful as we have known them."

TOM CURREN
(Three time world champion and founder of Surfrider Foundation Europe).

Surfing forms close relationships between surfers and their environment, an activity depending on such a subtle interactions of coastline, atmosphere and ocean, leaving no one indifferent. The surfer develops a sort of sea sense, to the point that he knows the ocean, feels it move under swell, wind and tide, comprehends its moods... and sometimes sees it suffer.
By regularly going into the ocean, the surfer can get even more exposed to pollution related risks.
Sore throats, ear infections, stomach bugs... at times pollution reminds passionate surfers that the ocean is not always as blue as it should be. Being stuck in bed is no fun, especially when convalescence coincides with a perfect swell.
Have you ever cancelled a session because of pollution? Have you ever bumped into floating rubbish? Ever seen the lineup overrun, not with surfers but with human waste? Nobody wants to ding a rail bumping into an oil drum. Without mentioning the material damages and costs, there is a real risk of injury.
Worse still are oil slicks, decimating marine life and forcing beach closures for months. Or unregulated coastal developments that make waves disappear.

There are so many factors that lead an otherwise individualistic surfer to consider the greater good, respect for others and for environments, developing a social conscience and sense of shared responsibility.
Respecting others does not only mean respecting the priority rules for etiquette and safety, it is also a way of safeguarding a clean playground for all.

HOW TO ACT AND PROTECT LOCALLY?

At an individual level, all our daily habits make a difference: Consuming wisely and sustainably, reducing waste, reusing and recycling, traveling clean, saving water and energy.
Where possible, opt for biking or walking as the best option to check the spot.
With simple, habitual acts we can limit our impact on the places we visit. The sand dunes in particular constitute a fragile ecosystem essential to the long term stabilization of the entire costal zone, meaning everybody should use designated paths to the beaches.
Of course, never leave waste behind and pick up some you find.
Set a good example to others around you. A good rule of thumb is to pick up your waste + 1 other.

There are a growing number of more environmentally friendly consumer products available to the surfer, vote with your wallet.

Always remember that surfing is only possible because nature makes it so.
To safeguard the natural environment in return is the least we can do.

Surfrider Foundation Europe
www.surfrider.eu

ASP: Association of Surfing Professionals, the body that governs professional surfing, crowning male and female world champions annually, in open, junior, and longboard divisions.

Backhand/backside: When a surfer rides with his back to the wave.

Barrel: Hollow part of the wave that the surfer rides through, also 'tube'.

Bodysurf: Riding waves without a board, usually with swim fins.

Bomb: A bigger set wave during any session, usually breaking further out, usually sought after by the best surfers.

Board shorts: Trunks adapted for surfing. Designed to limit rashes due to movement or friction with surfboard.

Bowl: A powerful hollow section of a wave, which throws more forward and less down the line. Often located on the final section of a wave i.e. 'the inside bowl'.

Charger: A brave, committed surfer with a preference for big or hollow waves.

Clean up set: A bigger than the average set of waves, breaking further out and leaving most surfers in the lineup caught inside ('cleaning them up').

Closeout: A wave breaking all at once across its length, as opposed to peeling.

Concave: Bottom of a surfboard hollowed out across its width from one rail to the other.

Dawn patrol: Sunrise surf session.

Double concave: Bottom of a surfboard hollowed out on each side of the stringer.

Double grab: Grabbing both rails at the same time.

Double up: When one wave catches up with another at the moment of breaking, adding power and steepness to the wave, usually making it barrel.

Drop in: When a surfer takes a wave already being ridden by another closer to the curl. Surfing's most offensive maneuver.

Epoxy: A surfboard made with epoxy resin and a polystyrene blank (EPS), as opposed to the conventional polyester/polyurethane (PU) construction. Mostly used in small wave boards to reduce weight.

Fade: A drop line cut towards the foam to get closer to the curl, e.g. faded (delayed) bottom turn. Also another word for dropping in ('to fade someone').

Fetch: Distance of ocean over which the wind blows creating a swell, one of three variables that govern swell height (with wind speed and wind duration).

Fin set up: Relates to the number of fins on a board e.g. single fin (one), twinnie (two), thruster (three), quad (four), etc.

Fin system: Fins that can be removed, useful for changing fin sizes and designs on the same board, and practical for traveling.

Fish: Wide, short, flat small wave design.

Flair: Anticipative skill instinct that helps a surfer take the best position into and through maneuvers.

Flow: Gracefulness on the wave between and through maneuvers.

Foam ball: Turbulent whitewater that travels laterally inside the tube.

Foot: Imperial unit of length (30.48cm) used to measure surfboards and waves.

Forehand/Frontside: When a surfer rides facing the wave.

Glass: Layer of fiberglass and resin covering the surfboard blank.

Glassy: Smooth, windless surf conditions.

Goofy foot: A surfer who rides right foot forward. A goofy foot rides lefts forehand, rights backhand.

Grab rail: Action of grabbing the board's rail, useful for tubes, airs and cutbacks.

Gun: Big wave surfboard.

Home break: Where a surfer regularly surfs and knows best.

ISA: International Surfing Association, recognized by the Olympic committee.

Kook: A derogatory term for a novice, someone not adhering to or unaware of the established surfing etiquette or conventions.

Leash: Polyurethane cord attaching the surfer and his board, attached above the back foot ankle.

Left: A wave that breaks from left to right looking out to sea.

Lien: Frontside air grabbing the heal side rail with the front hand.

Lineup: The zone just outside of where most waves are breaking, where surfers sit on their boards waiting for their next ride. In crowded lineups, a natural rotation and pecking order usually occurs.

Longboard: Surfboard over 9 feet long, usually designed for small waves with a wide tail and nose.

Mini mal: Shorter version of a longboard design.

Mute: Frontside air grabbing the toe side rail with the front hand.

Offshore: Wind blowing from land to sea.

Onshore: Wind blowing from sea to land.

Peak: Zone where the waves start breaking.

Pipeline: The world's most famous wave, located on the North Shore of Oahu, Hawaii. Last stop of the ASP Men's World Tour.

Polyester (PU): Oil-derived resin used to make surfboards, covering a polyurethane foam. The most common surfboard construction to date.

Pop: Action of making the surfboard tail release from the surface of the water to initiate getting it to slide or air.

Power surfing: When a surfer uses a lot of force on the rail to turn, throwing big spray.

Quad: Four fin surfboard design, has had a popularity renaissance in recent years.

Quiver: Collection of different surfboards at the surfer's disposal.

Reef boots: Rubber soled neoprene boots to protect against sharp coral reefs.

Regular foot: Surfer who rides left foot forward. The regular foot rides rights forehand, lefts backhand (also known as 'natural foot' in Australia).

Retro: Vintage surfboard design.

Rebound: Final stage of a roundhouse cutback where the surfer hits the breaking curl he is traveling back towards.

Right: Wave breaking from right to left looking out to sea.

Rocker: Curve of the surfboard from nose to tail.

Single fin: Surfboard with one fin, popular during the 1970's.

Session: Time spent in the waves.

Set: A group of waves breaking one after the other, preceded and followed by a lull.

Spot: A surf break, a place where surfing takes place.

Stance: Basic position of a surfer that determines whether he is goofy or regular foot. The gap between the feet is generally slightly more than shoulder width.

Switch foot: Inversion of stance.

Shaper: Surfboard designer and builder. He gives life to the board design by working on the foam blank, before it is glassed.

Stoked: When a surfer is filled with sensations of joy and pleasure.

Stringer: Thin wood reinforcement running through the blank from nose to tail to add strength.

Tail: Back of the board.

Tail pad: Traction device glued on the deck of the surfboard under the back foot. Allows better grip during radical maneuvers.

Thruster: Three finned surfboard, invented by Simon Anderson in 1981 and remains the standard high performance fin set-up to this day.

Timing: Synchronization of turns with the wave, to achieve maximum amplitude and performance.

Tow-in: Catching waves with a rope and jetski as opposed to paddling. In general, two surfers team up and alternate roles as jetski pilot and surfer.

Twin fin/twinnie: A surfboard with two fins, designed by four times world champion Mark Richards. Very popular from late 70's through to the early 80's, until the advent of the thruster.

Vee: 'V' shape across the width of the bottom of a surfboard, easing rail to rail transitions.

Wax: Wax applied over top of the surfboard for the feet to grip.

Wetsuit: Neoprene suit designed to keep surfers warm in cold water.

One More Wave...

Surfing is an open book.
Everyday, with each coming set, new lines are written, and new chapters unfold.

As a surfer, you have the rare privilege of getting close to nature, forging an intimate bond with the ocean.

The ocean will always be your best learning source.
Go surfing to develop this pure and unrivalled feeling, and stay close and dedicated to the amazing energy of ocean waves.

I hope this book will help to get you close to the curl and surfing's essence; that it will develop better balance on your board and in nature, that it will give you pleasure in discovering surfing culture. Above all, I hope that it will push you to get one more wave.
Riding waves is the best fun in the world, it's free and it will change your life.

Enjoy the ride.

INDEX

Art Direction : Emmanuel Batifoulier

Graphic design : Christophe Lestage

Color correction : ProfilKolor

Print : ONA-Spain

Publisher : Sandbar

First edition : October 2012

ISBN : 978-1-908520-99-9

CONTACTS

Bernard Testemale

brainshots@wanadoo.fr

www.testemale-photos.com

Didier Piter

didier.piter@wanadoo.fr

Art print available :

www.profilkolor.fr